JOB KILLERS

JOB KILLERS

How Government Regulation
Increases Unemployment and
The Solution to Get Americans Back to Work Now

Dan Sinas

iUniverse, Inc.
New York   Bloomington

iUniverse books may be ordered through booksellers or by contacting:

iUniverse
1663 Liberty Drive
Bloomington, IN 47403
www.iuniverse.com
1-800-Authors (1-800-288-4677)

ISBN: 978-1-4502-1057-7 (sc)
ISBN: 978-1-4502-1055-3 (hc)
ISBN: 978-1-4502-1056-0 (ebook)

Printed in the United States of America

iUniverse rev. date: 08/26/2010

Dedication

This book is dedicated to my wife, Susan. Her love, support and unending encouragement made it possible for me to complete this book.

Acknowledgements

I would like to acknowledge and thank the owners of The PR Companies (PRemployer, Inc., Personnel Resources, Inc. and PR Insurance, Inc.) for their ongoing support and generosity, and for forming the best team of professionals I have ever had the pleasure of working with.

The quote by Dr. Adrian Rogers is used by permission from Love Worth Finding Ministries. For additional resources and information, visit www.lwf.org

Nothing is easier than blaming others for our troubles and absolving ourselves of responsibility for our choices and our actions.

—Barack Obama, 2009

Contents

PROLOGUE

I was born and raised in Lansing, Michigan, the youngest of three children. My mother and father were both Greek, but born in the United States. All of my grandparents, however, immigrated to this country from Greece, arriving through Ellis Island in New York in the early 1900's. When they arrived in America, the only thing my grandparents possessed was a desire to live in a free country where they had a chance at making a life for themselves. None of them spoke any English; they had no job, very little money, no material wealth, and no one to provide for their needs. As was common for the immigrants migrating to the United States during that time, most of them would reside in common locations and cities, and much of the country was characterized by distinct ethnic communities of Irish, Greeks, Italians, and many others. They worshipped together, socialized together and supported each other while they were making a brand new life in a foreign land. They had to become self-sufficient, they relied on no government handouts to help them out, and their existence often consisted of nothing more than a day to day struggle to survive. Yet through such severe conditions, their hard work sustained them and provided hope that their lives in this new country would be better than what they left behind.

Soon after arriving in America, both of my grandfathers became small business owners. They didn't become rich by any means, but they earned a living and provided the basic necessities for their family. Thousands of other immigrants and millions of other Americans did the same. They relied upon nothing more than the sweat of their own brow, the understanding that not working meant not eating, and the realization that no one else was responsible for taking care of their needs. Life was a struggle, and hard work was the only way to overcome the hardships. Not all succeeded, many failed. It was the demands and challenges themselves that developed their character and instilled in them a sense that nothing in life is free, it has to be earned. The legacy of my grandparents was the belief that we must rely upon our own efforts in order to succeed and that personal sacrifice and hard work are necessary to achieve any improvement in life.

While growing up in Lansing in the sixties and seventies, our family was deeply entrenched in the Greek community, and it seemed that we did everything with fellow Greeks. I remember how the Greek Orthodox Church was very much the center of our existence, as we worshiped there, attended "Greek school" there, and held social events such as weddings, dances and festivals at the church. I spent a significant amount of time with fellow Greeks, and I thoroughly enjoyed the feeling of an ethnic identity. One of the things I clearly remember is listening to all the different stories of how each family came to the United States, and hearing about all the different ways a brand new life was started from scratch. It seemed everyone faced tremendous challenges that had to be overcome to carve out a sustainable existence in this country. I recall the stories of how difficult it was to arrive in a country unable to speak the language, but somehow able to obtain work or open a business. There was a common disdain for unnecessary handouts and undeserved charity, and they all seemed to take tremendous pride in the fact that they could become citizens of a country that allowed and encouraged personal success, but guaranteed nothing but the probability of continual struggle. There was a shared belief that the combination of integrity plus individual effort, plus ability, would equal deserved rewards.

That belief was passed on from my grandparents to my mother and father, who in turn attempted to instill the same beliefs in me and my brother and sister. But I didn't always take to the lessons of my parents very well, and that part about putting forth the required work and effort was one with which I often struggled. It was shortly after beginning college that I experienced the reality of that lesson first hand. I experienced what happens when you fail to work hard and don't put forth your best effort — you obtain your deserved reward, which in my case was a 0.0 in freshman algebra. And no matter how much I tried to convince my father that I just didn't understand the material, I knew that the real reason for my failure was my total lack of hard work and discipline, mainly my unwillingness to actually go to class on any regular basis. Up to that point, school was easy for me and I could skate by without having to put much into it. But college was different. Homework loads were massive, studying was essential, and going to class was absolutely necessary if you wanted to understand the subject matter. I did none of those to any significant degree and my failing grade was proof. The absence of concerted effort resulted in my due reward. And I could lay the blame at no one's feet but my own. I recall my father saying, "Son, if you really did attend class, turned in your homework and studied hard, I can't get upset at your failing grade. But I suspect otherwise. I will bet you did none of those things, and instead you thought that somehow you could get lazy, not study and still expect a decent grade. So you either have a serious math deficiency, or you're a fool…."

Ouch. I just experienced my first real life lesson as an adult. If you fail to work at anything, don't expect anything but failure. Don't try to make excuses or blame others. Take responsibility for your actions, and never expect to be given anything you didn't earn. Since graduating from school and entering the working world, I have witnessed first-hand how critical this principle is to both business success and employee advancement. As someone who has been in the human resources profession for over twenty-five years, I am constantly reminded of, and I constantly deal with, the fallout of what happens to businesses when employees refuse to put forth any discernable effort and fail to perform at required levels. Businesses that must deal with poor performers end up spending precious time and money trying to correct performance problems rather than direct efforts at helping the high achievers do better. I've dealt with employee performance issues on a daily basis, and I've done so in unionized businesses, non-union businesses, domestic operations, foreign locations, large Fortune 100 organizations, and very small privately owned businesses. I have had the pleasure of hiring thousands of employees, and have experienced the heartache and anguish of terminating thousands as well.

In my mind, the two most important aspects of business success are how employees perform and how companies manage employee performance. Those aspects are what determine whether a company turns a profit or loses money. They determine whether a company succeeds or fails. And if a business fails, every employee associated with that company suffers a devastating job loss. When businesses fail, wages are no longer paid, taxes are no longer collected, commerce is disrupted, and our economy as a whole is negatively impacted. Therefore, a skilled labor force, performing at required levels, leads to profitable businesses, and profitable businesses will help sustain our nation's economic activity and keep more employees working.

However, over the course of the last twenty years, I have witnessed some disturbing patterns that are affecting the workplace. Our schools continue to graduate students who are less and less prepared for the working world, and many lack the basic skills and knowledge necessary to perform at acceptable levels. More and more employees seem to embrace the idea that a job is a "right", not something that must be continually earned. The old concept that a strong work ethic is necessary to retain a job is being replaced by a new belief that it's acceptable to do just enough to keep from getting fired. And when employers choose to terminate employees because of poor performance or lack of effort, there are a multitude of laws and regulations enacted by our government that often allow those terminated individuals to obtain underserved protections and compensation. There has been a significantly increased role by our government in the workplace which has led to burdensome and often counter-productive mandates on businesses that negatively impact their performance. Although some government intervention in the workplace is justifiable when the basis for the intervention is to stop abuses and prevent harm, the trend over the last two decades has been to go far beyond that objective. The shift has been gradual, but steady and profound. The ever expanding influence government is demanding over the workplace is detrimental to our nations' economic future.

The overwhelmingly complex web of employment laws that regulate the workplace makes it extremely difficult for most employers to understand exactly what is required or prohibited. To remain compliant, employers must hire staff to handle the compliance efforts, or obtain such services and consultation from outside sources. Employment laws also allow employees to file charges against their employer for any alleged violations, so employers must be constantly prepared to defend themselves against those allegations. The existence of these regulations often acts to *encourage* employees to sue their employers, even when the employer acted reasonably and lawfully. Our legal system is structured in such a manner that it is exceedingly costly to defend a legal charge, so out-of-court settlement has become the preferred method of dispensing justice. But this only creates incentives for many individuals who have been justifiably terminated to nevertheless make allegations of employer illegalities. Regardless of the relative merits of the allegations, these actions force businesses to incur significant defense costs, and in an effort to mitigate these expenses, employers often must pay the terminated employee a sizable amount of money in return for dropping the charges. It is a form of legalized extortion.

Businesses are fighting a battle to stay alive, become profitable, remain competitive, and keep people employed. But our government keeps taking actions that are detrimental to business interests, and instead, are creating too many opportunities for undeserving employees to be protected. The cost associated with regulatory compliance, poor employee performance, and legal defense expenses equates to dollars that could otherwise be used to create more jobs, or pay higher wages to employees who work hard, perform well, and deserve every penny they make. Our regulatory policies are harming our businesses, our employees and our economy as a whole, and if continued, will lead to even further job erosion.

The late Dr. Adrian Rogers, former pastor of Bellevue Baptist Church in Memphis, Tennessee wrote:

> "Friend, you cannot legislate the poor into freedom by legislating the wealthy out of freedom. And what one person receives without working for, another person must work for without receiving. The government can't give to anybody anything that the government does not first take from somebody. And when half of the people get the idea that they don't have to work because the other half's going to take care of them, and when the other half gets the idea that it does no good to work because somebody's going to get what I work for. That, dear friend, is about the end of any nation." *(Source: This material is used by permission of Love Worth Finding Ministries; for additional resources and information, visit http://www.lwf.org/site/PageServer?pagename=lis_quote)*

Unfortunately, there are many who seem to be oblivious to this truth, especially politicians. They continue to offer 'solutions' that require hundreds of billions of dollars of taxpayer money to fund bailouts, buyouts and stimulus packages, only to watch these programs result in even higher unemployment. This country needs new solutions — ones that are effective. We need a new perspective on how to remove barriers to job creation and develop new ways to help businesses and employees prosper. We must re-evaluate the role government should play in the workplace, and realize that when government over-regulates the private sector, businesses suffer and jobs are jeopardized.

Over the course of the last twenty years, I have spoken to hundreds of business owners, executives, managers, human resource professionals and employees who all share this viewpoint, and it is from that perspective that this book is written.

THE CRITICAL ROLE
OF THE EMPLOYEE

After realizing that in order to stay in school I was going to have to actually study, go to class, and work hard at it, I finally got my act together. I eventually went on to graduate school and received a master's degree in labor and industrial relations from Michigan State University, got married, moved to Texas, and obtained my first job in Dallas working for TRW Optoelectronics Division. My job title was Human Resources Representative, and my primary responsibility was recruiting engineers and other professional employees. Attempting to learn what we actually made and how we made it, I asked one of the engineers who worked there if he could show me around and explain what we manufactured and how it was done. The products we made were essentially computer chips, infrared light-emitting diodes, and other microelectronic devices. I remember being shown how these devices were produced and wondering who had the brainpower to think of such amazingly technical things. During my plant tour, we came upon several areas where the engineer explained how just one little mistake made by an employee in the manufacturing process would result in thousands of computer chips being scrapped and deemed useless. Such an event would cost the company tens of thousands of dollars in lost revenue. One little mistake and the company would suffer serious financial repercussions.

It was an eye-opening experience that taught me the significant relationship between employee performance and business survival. Poor workmanship, lack of concentration, inadequate effort, insufficient training, poor execution, and failure to follow procedures all play a significant factor in whether a business makes a profit. It was then that I realized that my role as a recruiter was essential to our business, because finding, developing, and retaining the very best employees was the key to our company's success. It is just like in sports where teams that possess the greatest amount of talent and consistently demonstrate the strongest work ethic are the teams that regularly compete at the highest levels. In business, the collective skills and abilities of the employees in any given organization will determine whether the enterprise grows or contracts, whether it innovates or follows, and whether it operates profitably or at a loss. Any given business is nothing without employees—whether there are thousands or just one. It is people who make every decision, plot every strategy, execute every sale, create every product, and deliver every service. For every action a business takes, an individual or group of individuals was responsible. From the development of marketing strategies to the sweeping of the floors, such activities are performed by employees. Even when technology is prevalent in a certain business and robotic means are utilized to manufacture products or assist in the delivery of services, there are still humans behind the development of this technology, the programming of the machines, the decision to purchase the technology, and the determination of how it is to be deployed. There is no escaping the human element or the necessity of human influence in any given business activity. Therefore, it is safe to say, without employees, there will be no revenue generated, and without revenue, there can be no profits.

Conversely, human capital is also one of the highest cost elements in any business. Labor cost is normally the highest financial outlay, or, if not the highest, it is a close second to material cost. The cost to hire, train, compensate, develop, and manage a single employee is very high. The price for making hiring mistakes is also significant when you factor in the cost of errors, scrap, rework, production delays, service interruptions, and damaged customer relations. These expenses increase further when you factor in the cost it takes to rehire, retrain, and redevelop a new employee, plus the cost of going without a trained employee for whatever period of time it takes for new employees to become proficient in their position. Therefore, it is imperative that human resources strategies are focused on finding and retaining employees who add value to the organization, not cost. There is no guarantee that the contribution an employee makes to the bottom line surpasses the total cost of employing that individual. I've heard many people in business exclaim that employees are both assets and liabilities. I disagree with that view. I believe any given employee is either an asset *or* a liability. It's an either–or proposition. In every single employment relationship, in every single company, the employee is either adding value to the bottom line or adding nothing but cost. Determining which employees are value adders and which employees are cost drivers is the key to remaining competitive.

There is a third perspective from which to view the employee. Employees can also expose companies to significant legal liability. The myriad of employment laws, many of which will be subsequently discussed, create a tremendous amount of potential liability for the employer. The sheer number of employment laws that have been enacted, and the system of enforcement agencies to monitor the workplace, increases significantly the chances of being sued by a current, past, or prospective employee. Under any given employment law, the regulation *requires* the employer to engage in certain actions or behaviors, or *prohibits* the employer from engaging in certain actions or behaviors, and many times, they do both. Employees and applicants may sue their employers for any alleged violation of these laws, and often do so even when there has been no illegal conduct. The costs of defending employment claims are immense, and once the charges are filed, the business is forced to spend significant amounts of money to defend itself, regardless of its guilt or innocence. The system is tilted in favor of the employee by facilitating legal action against employers, yet provides little to no relief for employers when defending themselves against unfounded claims, frivolous lawsuits, and/or charges that have no merit. When a disgruntled employee—terminated for poor performance, unsatisfactory attendance, or any other justifiable reason—alleges illegalities, the employer must respond to these charges, invest a great deal of time and energy in crafting its response, and spend significant amounts of money trying to prove its actions were legal. If the employer "wins" and the charges are dropped, the employee simply walks away from the proceedings, without having suffered any financial loss. The "winner" has no means to recoup the monetary losses related to its defense and also faces the possibility of having to repair its image to its staff, associates, and customers.

Consider also the fact that employees essentially have "two bites at the apple" when it comes to charging an employer with wrongdoing. First, the employee can file a charge with the Equal Employment Opportunity Commission (EEOC) alleging discrimination. The EEOC then will begin an investigation into the charges by demanding from the defendant company the submission of records, files, statistics, position statements, and any additional documents they deem necessary to make a determination of the merits of the charge. This process can take anywhere from a couple months to a couple years. The EEOC can choose to sue the employer on behalf of the employee (or similarly situated employees), they can attempt some sort of settlement from the employer, or they can issue a "no cause" finding, meaning they will not pursue the matter any further. At this point, the EEOC issues a "right to sue" letter to the complainant, indicating the employee can pursue civil litigation through the courts by suing the employer on his own.

The employee, therefore, has two options: utilize a governmental regulatory agency to pursue a legal claim against an employer; or, if the governmental investigation results in no action against that employer (presumably for lack of evidence of any wrongdoing) the employee can then take those same allegations to an attorney. At this stage, the employee has the right to, once again, bring action against the employer, trying one more time to extract some financial settlement. If settlement demands don't bear enough fruit, the employee may elect to take the case to trial. Unlike our criminal justice system that prohibits an individual from being charged twice for the same offense under the "double jeopardy" rule, it's perfectly legal to file the same charges twice against an employer. Realize also that when attorneys take these cases, they almost always accept them on a contingency basis, meaning the employee pays nothing to the attorney unless there is an award or settlement in the favor of the employee. This means the employee has spent nothing to require the government to investigate the allegation of wrongdoing, and if that agency finds no wrongdoing on the part of the employer, the employee then has the second "double jeopardy" opportunity to utilize our court system for the same purpose, all the while not paying a single penny to get these charges pursued.

Unfortunately, the employer, on the other hand, has to spend thousands of dollars answering these charges, not just once to the government, but also in many cases a second time to the retained plaintiff's attorney. And if the employer "wins," they are still deep in the till paying to defend their actions, while the employee, who was a two-time "loser," has paid nothing ... not a single penny. This system is inherently unfair to the business owner as there are no possible financial repercussions for the employee if their case is found to be without merit, or even frivolous, not once, but twice. This unbalanced system does nothing but encourage and *facilitate* litigation. There is no apparent concern for the significant negative impact these legal proceedings have on employers, or the resulting damage incurred in terms of lost revenue, exorbitant expenses, demoralized staff, damaged image, and overall bitterness that boils when accused of something that is just not true. We have a system that basically says, "Go ahead and file a charge, or sue, because you have nothing to lose and much to gain." This is a purposely designed system that tilts the scales of justice against the employer and in favor of the employee.

Therefore, it is extremely important for a company to be continually mindful of the potential cost of noncompliance. There is an undeniable link between employees and the bottom line. The common denominator for business success, job growth, economic expansion, and generous tax receipts is a high-performing employee. Organizations that have the ability to recruit and retain top talent will be at an advantage. Just as critical, organizations must also have in place a system that facilitates the identification of poor performers who add cost, but no significant value to the business, and then eliminate them from the organization. When we understand the relationship between employee performance and business success, and when we understand the link between business success and economic vitality, we should be driven to formulate policy at the national level that encourages businesses to hire and retain top-level performers. We should also have a system of laws that do not act as barriers to businesses that wish to eliminate employees who underperform. Unfortunately, that is exactly what is *not* happening. Government has assumed a much more active role in the workplace and has continued to steadily increase its intervention in the private sector over the last twenty years. While some of the laws that have been enacted are reasonable, many are excessively far-reaching, overly complex, and counterproductive to business productivity and economic performance. But it is evident that Congress does not see things quite that way.

THE PENDULUM

Government intervention in the workplace is expanding at an ever-increasing rate, and the legislation that has been passed over the last twenty years has been increasingly burdensome on businesses, especially small businesses. Such laws have the effect of curtailing the rights of the business owner to hire, fire, and utilize the employees in a manner that best suits the needs of the business. There is a need for certain legal restraints on employers, and I am in no way advocating the elimination of employment laws or proposing we give businesses unencumbered rights to do as they please. But there needs to be a balance. We should enact laws that protect employees from abuse and exploitation, while at the same time provide businesses with protections from unnecessary governmental interference that acts to harm the ability to be profitable. The pendulum of regulation needs to be centered, neither too inclined to protect employees nor too inclined to protect businesses. When the pendulum swings too far to the side of business, the likelihood of abuse and exploitation by the employer increases, which exposes employees to potentially harmful behaviors. When the regulatory pendulum swings too far to the side of employees, undeserving individuals frequently obtain undue financial gains, and businesses are often forced to incur the cost of burdensome legal proceedings, unnecessary litigation, and steep legal defense expenses. Neither of these extremes is beneficial to our nation's workplace or our nation's economy.

If we look at the historical record of congressional activism in the workplace, we see where there were many instances where employment laws were indeed necessary to curtail abuse and exploitation of the worker. Looking back in our country's history, we find many different ways in which the workplace has been structured and managed, and we see varying degrees of government intervention and control. If one was to view the relationship of the extent of government control against the freedom of the business owner to do as he or she pleases, they are in inverse proportion. The more the government intervenes, the less the business owner controls. For example, total absence of government control or intervention in the workplace would be what characterized slavery. There were no restraints on the business owner over his employees. As a matter of fact, slaves were not even considered employees but property to be bought and sold as the owner deemed necessary. Eventually, such abusive and abhorrent work relationships were eradicated and made illegal. It is certainly an example of the type of governmental intervention that was not only necessary, but morally justified on all fronts. We as a nation could simply not allow the enslavement of other human beings. Making such practices illegal was the only way to eradicate slavery, and we were right and just to do so. It was also the beginning of the notion that if governmental intervention worked to eradicate an insidious practice such as slavery, then government could also be used to effectuate other changes in the workplace that are deemed morally reprehensible practices as well, and that became the standard used to justify passage of future laws that further regulated the workplace.

Decades later, the Industrial Revolution was beginning to transform America in ways that were never imagined. We were steadily shifting from an agrarian culture to an industrialized economy. There was massive migration from rural areas to urban centers where jobs were abundant. The early decades of the 1900s brought us innovative manufacturing systems and mass production capabilities that required employment of thousands of employees in the auto, steel, construction, and related industries. This workforce migration, however, soon led to our next moral outrage: the abusive work practices and exploitation of the blue-collar worker. Long work hours, unsafe and insufferable working conditions, low wages, lack of benefits, frequent workplace injuries or fatalities, and exploitation of child labor soon became associated with the business world.

In response to these horrible working conditions, the birth of unions sprang forth. Collective action against abusive employers was viewed as the only way to protect employee interests. The labor movement was volatile, often violent, and frequently combative. Most employers wanted nothing to do with unions, as they were viewed as threats to production and profits. Union sympathizers were labeled communists, radicals, extremists, troublemakers, traitors, thugs, and thieves. Labor disputes often ended with strong-arm tactics and violent actions against employees, and workers were often fired, beaten, or killed if they were involved in the labor movement. Significant portions of the business community were engaging in reprehensible actions that were being viewed as morally repugnant as were the slave owners' actions.

Popular sentiment began to turn against the business community and in favor of the workers' plight, and government was once again relied upon to intervene to end abusive workplace conditions and practices. New laws were enacted, such as the National Labor Relations Act (NLRA) in 1935, which has been the cornerstone of labor-management relations ever since. Congress enacted the NLRA to protect the rights of employees, to establish ground rules for contract negotiations, and to curtail certain labor and management practices. The unions were successful in establishing the notion of "workplace justice," and unions did serve a very useful purpose. They were able to shine a light on business practices that were exploitative or unjust. Unions were instrumental in getting employees protection from unsafe working conditions; they helped eradicate child labor abuses; and they were able to secure for their members higher wages, paid time off, retirement benefits, and protection from arbitrary employment actions.

The NLRA and unions were the seeds that spawned the growth of regulatory controls over the workplace. Justification for government action was widely accepted if it stopped abusive practices against employees. As time marched on and the workplace and workforce grew, there was a growing movement to afford more and more protections to employees, and more and more restraint on employers. There are now dozens of governmental agencies and regulatory bodies overseeing a multitude of employment laws. According to the U.S. Department of Labor website, there are now over 180 federal laws that cover over 10 million employers and over 125 million employees. And that's not counting the thousands of state and local employment laws currently in force.

However, as more and more employment laws were added to the books, it became evident that the standard for enacting laws shifted from an attempt to protect employees from *exploitation* to a standard of providing for employees' *personal needs*. As government reaches further and further into the private-sector business world, it continues to formulate laws that can no longer be justified by moral outrage. We now find Congress enacting workplace laws that regulate every aspect of the employment relationship, including how employers interview, select, assign, pay, discipline, train, and terminate employees, as well as how leave policies, benefit plans, and retirement funding is to be handled. To provide an understanding of the extent of the workplace regulations, here are just a *fraction* of the over 180 federal workplace laws that are currently in effect:

- FLSA: Fair Labor Standards Act mandates minimum wages and salary levels, determines what constitutes work time for purposes of calculating pay, requires overtime pay for certain employees, and restricts child labor.
- ERISA: Employee Retirement Income Security Act sets minimum standards (including notice requirements) for establishing, administering, and maintaining certain employee benefit plans.
- FCRA: Fair Credit Reporting Act requires employers to provide notice and get consent before getting a credit report or other types of background or investigative reports on employees or applicants; it requires employers to give certain information to employees or applicants before taking negative action based on a report; and it establishes standards employers must follow to destroy consumer records.
- FMLA: Family and Medical Leave Act requires employers with fifty or more employees to give eligible employees up to twelve weeks of unpaid leave per year, with continued health benefits, for the birth or placement of a child, to care for a family member with a serious health condition, or to recuperate from their own serious health condition. Eligible employees must have worked for the employer for one year

and worked a minimum of 1250 hours in the previous 12 months.

- WHCRA: Women's Health and Cancer Rights Act provides protections for individuals who elect breast reconstruction in connection with a mastectomy.
- HIPAA: Health Insurance Portability and Accountability Act governs insurance for people with preexisting conditions and provides additional opportunities to enroll in a group health plan if you lose other coverage or experience certain life events. It requires medical information be kept private and restricts which individuals may access personal medical information.
- FUTA: Federal Unemployment Tax Act authorizes the Internal Revenue Service to collect a federal employer tax used to fund state workforce agencies.
- SUTA: State Unemployment Tax Act is a payroll tax, and each state requires employers to pay a tax rate for each employee. It is used solely for the payment of unemployment benefits to eligible unemployed workers.
- COBRA: Consolidated Omnibus Budget Reconciliation Act requires employers to provide continued group health insurance coverage for up to thirty-six months to employees (and possibly their spouses and dependents) who would otherwise lose coverage.
- FICA: Federal Insurance Contribution Act is an employment tax imposed by the federal government on both employees and employers to fund Social Security and Medicare.
- Title VII: Title VII of the Civil Rights Act of 1964 prohibits discrimination on the basis of race, color, national origin, religion, and sex in every aspect of employment.
- ADEA: Age Discrimination in Employment Act forbids age discrimination against people who are age forty or older.
- ADA: Americans with Disabilities Act prohibits discrimination against qualified employees with disabilities and requires employers to make reasonable accommodations for employees and applicants with disabilities.

- CRA: Civil Rights Act of 1866 prohibits discrimination on the basis of race in the making or enforcement of contracts, which includes every aspect of the employment relationship.
- IRCA: Immigration Reform and Control Act prohibits discrimination on the basis of citizenship and national origin in every aspect of employment and requires employers to verify that employees are authorized to work in the United States and keep records to that effect.
- PDA: Pregnancy Discrimination Act prohibits discrimination on the basis of pregnancy or childbirth in every aspect of employment and requires employers to treat pregnant women who are temporarily unable to work the same way they treat workers who are temporarily disabled for other reasons.
- EPA: Equal Pay Act requires employers to give male and female employees equal pay for doing equal work.
- NLRA: National Labor Relations Act regulates the relationship of employers and unions, prohibits employers and unions from engaging in unfair labor practices, and protects employees who engage in concerted activities to improve working terms and conditions, whether the workplace is unionized or not.
- WPA: Whistleblower Protection Act protects federal whistle-blowers or persons who work for the government who report agency misconduct.
- OWBPA: Older Workers Benefit Protection Act prohibits age discrimination in the provision of benefits, explains the criteria to be used in determining whether equal benefits have been provided, and requires employers to include particular language in waivers of an employee's right to sue for age discrimination.
- VEVRAA: Vietnam Era Veterans' Readjustment Assistance Act of 1974 requires federal contractors and subcontractors with government contracts of ten thousand dollars or more to take affirmative action to employ and promote qualified veterans of the Vietnam era and disabled veterans.
- WARN: Worker Adjustment and Retraining Notification Act requires certain sized employers to give sixty days' notice to

employees who will lose their jobs through large layoffs or plant closings, with limited exceptions.
- OSHA: Occupational Safety and Health Act requires employers to comply with workplace safety and health standards.
- HAZCOM: Hazard Communications Act/Employee Right-to-Know requires public employers to provide their employees with specific information and training on the hazardous chemicals to which employees may be exposed in the workplace.

There are also numerous other ways employers can be sued under legally recognized principals of:

- wrongful termination: providing for financial damages for terminations that are deemed unjust or unfair.
- retaliation: providing for financial damages if an employer is deemed to have taken any adverse employment actions against an employee who has charged the employer with wrongdoing.
- sexual harassment: using a position of authority (e.g., manager or supervisor) to obtain sexual favors; creating a work environment that is hostile or intimidating due to sexual behaviors, communications, or utterances.
- negligent hiring: not performing due diligence when hiring an employee, and overlooking certain factors that should have been considered before employing an individual.
- negligent retention: retaining an employee who is deemed to be a potential danger to other employees or the general public.
- defamation: making false statements about an employee that has the effect of damaging his reputation or ability to obtain other employment.
- breach of contract: violating contractual obligations.
- constructive discharge: quitting a job under duress; employment conditions that are considered so severe that they force an employee to quit rather than be subjected to such practices.

- intentional infliction of emotional distress: employer-caused emotional distress of the employee due to unjust employment actions or behaviors.
- fraud and negligent misrepresentation: purposefully providing false information regarding an employee, past or present.
- public policy violations: terminating employees because they reported illegal or unethical behavior by the employer, engaged in legally protected activity, and/or participated in a legal proceeding.

As you can see, we have gone well beyond providing employees basic human rights, which have been addressed in the National Labor Relations Act, the Civil Rights Act, and Title VII. Our government has found it necessary to venture into areas, such as mandated time off, mandated compensation levels, mandated pay for being unemployed, mandated retirement benefits, mandated immigration enforcement, mandated benefits extension to ex-employees, and so on. As Thomas Jefferson once said, "Government big enough to supply everything you need is big enough to take everything you have.... The course of history shows that as a government grows, liberty decreases." Nevertheless, certain members of Congress, the courts, and the labor unions have, over the last twenty years, painted businesses as the deep-pockets exploiters of employees, not the providers of jobs, pay, benefits, or a way of life. Congress adds laws to the books that give employees more of the business owners' pie seemingly without regard to how it impacts the business's ability to compete and realize a profit. If employees benefit from such laws and obtain more for no more effort, so be it. It's Congress's view that employees should have more, and the business owner should be required to provide more, even if it will be detrimental to the health of the enterprise. Many members of Congress show little regard for how such mandates affect the operation of a business, impact the financial performance, or affect the business's ability to survive. And what a deal for the employees—they just call on politicians to mandate privileges to them without a required analysis of whether the business has the ability to actually pay for them. Therefore, employees reap the rewards, businesses pay, and the politicians get the credit for improving the individual condition. So the governmental machine keeps enacting laws that further encroach on the business owner's rights, and our government is fully prepared to keep this system churning in an effort to gain political favor with employees, garner the all-important vote, and hold onto political power with a firm grasp.

This is not to suggest that the business community is not without its bad actors and rotten apples. The recent revelations of massive corruption at organizations, such as Enron, Adelphia Communications, HealthSouth, Global Crossing, Tyco, and WorldCom, are proof that businesses do and will engage in abhorrent practices. Such behaviors can never be justified under any analysis, but Congress often uses these examples to enact further restrictions on the business community as a whole. However, most businesses do not engage in widespread abuses and most operate under the rule of law and abide by these mandates. Big business is often used as a metaphor for corruption, and further regulatory controls are the answer to stopping corruption. However, most businesses are small, employing less than five hundred employees. According to data from the U.S. Department of Commerce, the U.S. Bureau of Census, and the U.S. Department of Labor, in 2008 there were 29.6 million businesses in the United States. Small firms with less than 500 employees represent 99.9 percent of those 29.6 million businesses. Large businesses are estimated to number only 18,000.

But almost every workplace law on the books applies to businesses with merely fifteen or more employees. Most small businesses do not have the financial resources to hire staff attorneys and human resources professionals, and they can't afford to keep lobbyists fighting for their cause. The laws that they are subjected to, however, require someone in the organization to possess specialized training to understand all of the various laws' provisions, requirements, and prohibitions. Even in the law profession, attorneys will readily admit that to best understand employment law and be most effective for their clients, lawyers must devote their whole practice to nothing but employment law. But Congress expects businesses, especially small businesses, to be able to understand and abide by laws that even lawyers can't understand unless they deal with such on a continual basis. To do so requires more financial outlays from the business owner to lawyers, consultants, advisers, and the like just to attempt to remain in compliance with the multitude of employment laws on the books. Congress needs to have a much deeper understanding of how their legislative products impact the small business owner and how difficult it can be to comply with the confusing, technical, and complicated laws that they enact.

For example, we have workplace regulations that, conceptually, seem to be admirable, such as the Family Medical Leave Act (FMLA). On the surface, FMLA appears to be the fair thing to do: provide up to twelve weeks of unpaid leave to employees in the event they (or a family member) have a serious medical condition or are adopting or expecting a child. But dig deeper, and the law goes into the unreasonable mode when it mandates that such leave can be broken down into tiny little bits of time called "intermittent leave" where employees can take a day here, an hour there, thirty minutes here, fifteen minutes there, and so on, up to *the equivalent of twelve weeks*. The employer must track such intermittent leave to the smallest increment of time that is normally used to track hours worked. These burdensome time-tracking requirements force employers to keep records of when an employee took an hour for a doctor's appointment or had to arrive fifteen minutes late due to attendance to their therapy session, and then determine when such time has totaled up to twelve weeks. In other words, Congress showed little to no concern for how their regulations wreak havoc on the workplace. Scheduling proper manpower levels becomes extremely difficult, if not impossible, and providing coverage for those absences is very costly. Employees often give their employer little to no notice that they need to utilize intermittent leave, but they are legally protected from adverse employment actions and can file charges against the employer if such requests are denied. I have personally dealt with a situation where an employee, diagnosed with migraine headaches, was allowed to call the company any morning she experienced headaches, stipulate that the condition was FMLA-related, and then report to work when the headaches subsided. We never knew if she would arrive fifteen minutes late, two hours late, or be out the whole day. We would have to record each minute she was out and keep track of such time when calculating her allowed twelve weeks of leave each year. It was quite disruptive to the business and often resulted in critical work having to be reassigned to a less skilled employee or not getting done at all. We would experience a loss of revenue every time she was absent or late. The law states that such leave is "unpaid" but fails to consider that the granting of such leave is extremely disruptive to operations and costly to the business. The law also allows the employee to repeat this pattern of job-protected leave every year, regardless of how disruptive it becomes for co-workers or how damaging it is on business operations and profitability.

If Congress had given due consideration to the effect this law had on businesses, it might have instead required the employer to provide a certain amount of "instances" the employee can be away from work due to medical circumstances. For example, twelve weeks of a standard five-day workweek equals sixty days. Write the law so that it says employees are allowed sixty *instances* of time away from work, regardless of whether the amount of time is a whole day, a half-day, or twenty minutes away from work. Period. By that approach, Congress looks at the needs of the employee balanced against the needs of the business. They would have effectively given the employee some needed time away from work, protected their job, but not saddled the employer with ridiculous time-tracking mechanisms, unpredictable numbers of absences, and costly disruptions to revenue generation. It doesn't solve all of the inconveniences the employer still must deal with, but at least it gives some consideration to how businesses actually operate.

Let's examine yet another example of the complex and confusing legislation that Congress imposes upon businesses. The Americans with Disabilities Act (ADA) was passed into law in 1990 and was intended to eliminate discriminatory treatment against individuals with physical or mental impairments. The major tenets of the law basically state that it shall be illegal for an employer to discriminate against any individual with a disability if the disabled person can perform the essential function of the job, with or without reasonable accommodation. I believe it is a justifiable cause to attempt to eradicate discrimination against disabled individuals. But this law is another prime example of how worthwhile endeavors are tarnished when Congress attempts to regulate the workplace by formulating legalistic and confusing legislation. A closer look at this law reveals that the term "disability" means, with respect to an individual: (1) a physical or mental impairment that substantially limits one or more of the major life activities of such individual, (2) a record of such an impairment, or (3) being regarded as having such impairment.

The law is complex and leaves many questions unanswered. Most employers struggle with trying to determine whether employees with a "condition" meet the definition of a disability and whether they could be deemed qualified for a particular position based upon their ability to perform the essential functions of the job, with or without reasonable accommodation. Often, employers engage in tortured analysis of disability claims by employees who say their particular condition is a protected disability under the law, but the company disagrees with their assertion. To further complicate the issue, when employers have questions regarding whether their employees' medical condition meets the definition of disability, Congress forbids the employer from communicating directly with the employees' physician to get clarifying information, forcing the employer to communicate with the doctor only in writing. This only adds to the difficulty in working with the employee to try to determine possible accommodations, and it hinders the employer's ability to understand the exact nature of the medical condition of the employee. But Congress feels that type of information is too personal to let employers have access to it. Needless to say, these questions, more often than not, have to be answered by the courts to determine whether discriminatory conduct has occurred.

More than nineteen years since the enactment of ADA, employers, employees, and the courts are still wrestling with the questions of whether someone is indeed disabled under the law and how disabilities can and should be accommodated. It is yet another example of burdensome regulations that often require massive legal cost outlays by the employer to determine if they are properly complying with the law. To add to the confusion, the definition of "disability," "reasonable accommodation," "essential functions," "major life activities," "substantially limits," and "regarded as disabled" all have been viewed differently by different courts, who are trying to interpret the intentions of Congress. The whole aspect of "regarded as having impairment" is, to me, the most troubling. This portion of the law requires that the same basic protections be afforded to employees with *perceived* disabilities as those with actual ones. But the courts have recognized the inherent difficulty in determining whether an employer actually "regarded" an individual as disabled. An individual is regarded as disabled if the individual:

- has a physical or mental impairment that does not substantially limit major life activities, but is treated by a covered entity as constituting such limitation;
- has a physical or mental impairment that substantially limits major life activities only as a result of the attitudes of others toward such impairment;
- is treated by a covered entity as having a substantially limiting impairment.

(Source: C.F.R. § 1630.2(l) (1)–(3))

If you are as confused as I am, join thousands of others who struggle with this section of the statute. By interjecting the "regarded as" provision, we are witnessing the government enacting laws that regulate our *thought processes*. How we "perceive" individuals or how we "regard" them is now under legal scrutiny. It is troubling to say the least, and it is no wonder why so many employers are so confused and frustrated by these cumbersome and onerous laws.

But Congress was still not finished. In 2008, Congress passed, and President George W. Bush signed into law, the ADA Amendments Act (ADAAA), with a stated intent of clarifying some of the provisions of the law that were subject to confusion. These actions were also taken in response to the courts beginning to narrow their interpretation of what they considered to be disabilities under the law, and they began to rule more in favor of the employers. So Congress felt compelled to act to insure employees were not being unduly prevented from obtaining protections under the law. The ADAAA subsequently broadened the definitions of disability, allowed more medical conditions to be considered disabilities, and made it easier for employees and applicants to initiate legal actions against employers. In response to the amended law, the EEOC has indicated that the "regarded as" definition of the law would also be clarified as follows:

> Employers may commit "regarded as disabled" discrimination if they perceive someone as disabled, regardless of whether the employer believes the condition substantially limits a major life activity.

Unfortunately, I find this clarification needing more clarity. The original ADA was already exceedingly complex. The new ADAAA does nothing to reduce the complexity or simplify the definition of disability, and it even expands the legal protections to individuals with medical conditions, such as high blood pressure and carpal tunnel syndrome, even though the EEOC admits that some of those conditions may be disabilities for some but not others. It is expected that the only way that these new provisions will be sorted out is through further litigation.

However, instead of letting up on formulating more legislation that governs the workplace, Congress is getting even more aggressive in their desire to enact further mandates on businesses. Following is a summary of certain laws that have been proposed in the 111th Congress. It does not include healthcare reform or legislation that was proposed in prior sessions in 2008. (Source: www.govtrack.us/ and D. Albert Brannen; Fisher and Phillips, LLP)

- FMLA Inclusion Act (H.R. 2132): Would amend FMLA to permit leave to care for same-sex spouse, domestic partner, parent-in-law, adult child, sibling, or grandparent with serious health condition.
- Family and Medical Leave Enhancement Act of 2009 (H.R. 824): Would amend FMLA to:
  o cover employees at work sites employing fewer than fifty employees, but not fewer than twenty-five employees.
  o allow employees to take, as *additional* leave, parental involvement leave to participate in or attend children's and grandchildren's educational and extracurricular activities.
  o clarify that leave may be taken for routine family and medical needs, to assist the elderly relatives, and other purposes.
  o allow employees to elect, or employers to require, substitution of any paid family leave or paid sick leave for any FMLA leave.
- Family Fairness Act of 2009 (H.R. 389): Would amend FMLA to eliminate requirement that employees must work at least 1250 hours during the 12-month period before requesting

FMLA, thereby providing FMLA leave to part-time as well as full-time employees.

- Healthy Families Act (H.R. 2460): Would allow employees to earn one hour of paid sick leave for every thirty hours worked to address their own health needs and health needs of their families. Employers would begin accruing sick leave when employed and may begin using leave after sixty days. Phased-in coverage would eventually cover employers with twenty-five or more employees.
- Emergency Influenza Containment Act (H.R. 3991): Would mandate employers provide up to five paid sick days for a worker sent home or directed to stay home by the employer for a contagious illness, such as the H1N1 flu virus.
- Paid Vacation Act of 2009 (H.R. 2564): Would amend the Fair Labor Standards Act to require employers to provide a minimum of one week paid vacation to employees.
- Title VII Fairness Act (S. 166): Would amend the Americans with Disabilities Act and Title VII to delay start of time for filing charges of employment discrimination until aggrieved person has, or should be expected to have, enough information to support reasonable suspicion of discrimination.
- Working Families Flexibility Act (so-called "Union of One" law) (H.R. 1274): Would authorize an employee to request from an employer a change in the terms and conditions of the employee's employment if the request relates to:
  o the number of hours the employee is required to work.
  o the times when the employee is required to work.
  o where the employee is required to work.
- Employee Non-Discrimination Act of 2009 (H.R. 2981): Would amend Title VII to prohibit employment discrimination on the basis of sexual orientation or gender identity.
- Equal Employment for All Act (H.R. 3149): Would amend the Fair Credit Reporting Act to prohibit the use of consumer credit checks against prospective and current employees as a factor in making adverse employment decisions. Exceptions would allow them to be used if the job involves national

security, FDIC clearance, or positions of "significant financial responsibility," such as bank manager, loan officer, or financial manager. This bill would also prohibit employers from asking applicants to submit to voluntary credit checks.

- Employee Free Choice Act (H.R. 1409; S 560): Would amend the National Labor Relations Act to provide for:
  o elimination of secret-ballot elections.
  o arbitrator-mandated contract terms.
  o union-friendly bargaining rules.
  o increased penalties against employers.
  o more NLRB injunctions.
- Patriot Corporations of America Act (H.R. 1874): Would provide federal contracting preferences for, and a reduction in the rate of income tax imposed on, "Patriot" corporations. Among other requirements, employers would have to waive their Section 8(c) free speech rights and not oppose unionization of their employees to be considered a "Patriot" employer.
- Taxpayer Responsibility, Accountability, and Consistency Act of 2009 (H.R. 3269): Would make it more difficult for employer to misclassify a worker as an independent contractor and significantly increase penalties for misclassification. Penalties for intentional misclassification could be as high as three million dollars per year.

It is evident that Congress has no intention of backing off from their encroachment into private-sector workplaces. Much political hay can be made by enacting employee-friendly legislation, and politicians can tell their constituents that they are on the side of the working man. It has become politically advantageous to propose more "protections" for employees and to mandate that employers consider the employees' personal needs and individual misfortunes when formulating workplace policies and work rules. As noted above, Congress feels that it is not enough to require employers to provide their employees with medical leave for their own medical condition; they now want to pass a bill that mandates that employees be allowed to take job-protected leave for the medical condition of grandparents, adult children, in-laws, siblings, and same-sex partners. With the outbreak of "swine flu," Congress wasted no time in proposing yet another law that will dictate how employers must handle situations when an employee contracts a virus. The depths to which Congress will go to allow employees *not* to be at work are seemingly endless. Even though the business owner is engaged in private enterprise and is solely responsible for the financial performance of the company, government has increasingly intervened in the workplace and now wishes to further dictate how the business owner is to utilize his manpower and his capital.

Congress ignores the very fact that in order for employers to be able to compete for talented labor, they must, *on their own*, adopt competitive pay practices and leave policies. Free-market forces will dictate which companies employees wish to work for, and employers who are unwilling or unable to provide attractive working conditions will not be able to acquire the necessary employee talent. Nonetheless, decisions regarding pay levels, benefit offerings, and leave policies should be solely in the hands of the business owner, not the government. The legislative pendulum is apparently never swinging back toward the middle where it can balance the interests of employees and employers. It is indicative of how many of our elected officials seem to be unconcerned with the fact that excessive workplace regulation can break the backs of small businesses that employ so many of our nation's employees and threaten the job security of millions of Americans. They seem to have forgotten that free markets, private enterprise, and limited government are the foundations of our very economic system.

But that's the problem with governmental intervention in the workplace: once that train leaves the station, it loses its brakes.

CAPITALISM REDEFINED

Nowhere in the Constitution are we guaranteed a right to a wage-paying job. We are guaranteed the freedom to live our lives without overreaching governmental interference. We are free to pursue whatever vocation, trade, profession, or career we deem in our best interest. The founding fathers were wise in their insistence that true liberty can only be found when government is restrained and its reach is limited. Private property rights and unobtrusive government were the bedrock of the Declaration of Independence and the Constitution. The Tenth Amendment to the Constitution sates:

> The powers not delegated to the United States by the Constitution, nor prohibited by it to the States, are reserved to the States respectively, or to the people.

The Fourteenth Amendment states, in part, that:

> No State shall make or enforce any law which shall abridge the privileges or immunities of citizens of the United States: nor shall any State deprive any person of life, liberty or property, without due process of law; nor deny to any person within its jurisdiction the equal protection of the laws.

Our capitalistic system is based upon the notion of a "free market" where commerce is conducted between private owners of businesses, without any undue interference by the government in that free market. Those individuals who wish to start a business are free to do so and are solely responsible for raising and investing the necessary capital to start such an enterprise. Along with the right to invest private capital in any given business is the "right" to fail. No one is guaranteed success. No business is granted perpetuity. No business owner is shielded from financial devastation. But most importantly, government must be restrained from encroaching, to any significant degree, on the free-market system or unduly interfere with private enterprise. Supreme Court Justice Louis Brandeis aptly stated:

> the makers of the Constitution conferred, as against the government, the Right to be let alone; the most comprehensive of rights, and the right most valued by civilized men (*Olmstead v. United States*, 277 U.S. 438 (1928)).

Inherent in a capitalistic economic system is the principal of private ownership of land, capital, equipment, and intellectual property. The appropriate role for government is that of an oversight capacity, restricted to preventing illegal activity that would result in a crippling of free-market forces. Government, in other words, is like the referee in a football game. The referee's goal is to insure that the game is played according to the rules and that neither team has an undue advantage over the other. Yet allowing undue advantages is exactly what the government is doing steadily and deliberately when it comes to the interests of employees taking precedent over the rights and interests of employers. But without the business owner, our capitalistic system suffers greatly due to the absence of an economic engine that powers it. From that engine, economic activity is generated, capital flows freely, labor is traded for compensation, and compensation is traded for other goods and services, which generates further business development, and so on. Nowhere in that dynamic do you see a need for significant governmental intervention for it to survive. Nevertheless, we have let government not only intervene, but overreach in such a way as to cause our capitalistic system to be transformed into a nearly unrecognizable form of massive regulatory controls.

When government overreaches into the operation of the enterprise itself, it often results in converting the business into an inefficient, ineffective, unproductive, costly, and unprofitable operation. This results in one of three possible scenarios:

1. Jobs must be eliminated in order to shed costs.
2. The business must relocate to parts of the country (or world) that offer lower operating costs.
3. The business must close because number 1 or 2 above failed to produce the needed reversal of its financial collapse.

The government does not create profits; it confiscates them through taxes and it reduces them through burdensome regulatory controls and mandated employment practices. Diminishing profit levels contribute directly to job elimination. As jobs begin to disappear, so do tax revenues that are necessary to sustain our infrastructure. As income tax revenues begin to shrink, business taxes are often increased to make up for the shortfall. But the payment of taxes is not at issue; it is the payment of *excessive* and *unnecessary* taxes that contributes to business failures. Regulatory oversight is also not at issue; it is *excessive* and *overreaching* governmental control of the workplace that undermines business growth. Yet the government, still justifying its activism based upon the workplace of the 1930s, finds it necessary to dictate not only the taxes the business must pay, but it also assumes the authority to mandate how businesses are to pay their employees, how they should interview and hire them, how they should accommodate them, how they should terminate them, how much time off to provide them, how they should keep files on them, how they should retire them (and not to be overlooked), how businesses should pay monetary damages to employees if the government has deemed that a company has violated any of these complicated workplace regulations.

But Congress seems unconcerned about how businesses truly operate and acts as if they have no clue about what challenges businesses face. They either have never experienced or seem to have forgotten what it takes to run a for-profit business, and they don't understand the challenges of having to make payroll in the face of significantly declining revenue. Politicians spend other people's money that is collected through taxation, not earned by their own efforts. Government normally operates in a deficit mode, and when more money is needed to fund various projects, taxes are raised or more money is printed. Cutting spending to meet revenue shortfalls should be a priority over raising taxes. But politicians have either never experienced or seem to have forgotten how difficult it is to keep a business profitable and competitive against fierce competition. Businesses must operate under the requirement that revenue must exceed expenses, or else face extinction. Politicians are never held to that same standard and are seemingly oblivious to the fact that businesses are what provide people with jobs, and jobs are what keep the economy healthy. Yet they continually introduce legislation that interferes with that dynamic.

The common denominator of employment laws is that they allow employees to sue their employers, even when the company was completely justified in their employment decisions. Even though the employer acted reasonably, once a charge is filed by the employee, the company must incur significant cost in defending its actions. From a financial point of view, court cases are much more costly to the plaintiff's and defense attorneys because such cases require much greater amounts of time to prepare for litigation. Deposition costs are incurred, time is spent reviewing pertinent records, files, and documents, witnesses must be tracked down, and detailed preparations must be made to try the case in the courtroom. If the employer calculates that he will spend tens of thousands of dollars, if not more, taking it to court, settlement for something less than that begins to look like the prudent financial decision. The check is cut, but the employer, more times than not, finds himself paying an employee who was never treated improperly and deserves nothing financially from the employer. We long ago began this encroachment on employers' rights to be free from burdensome regulation, and we have continually whittled away at the employer's ability to manage their respective businesses without having to defend every action or decision it makes to some regulatory body, lawyer, judge, or jury.

There must be a concerted effort to look at the workplace rationally and realize it serves *everyone's* best interest to have a system that provides employees with certain rights, along with the employer's right to determine what strategies, plans, and employees are best suited to its needs so as to insure the survival of the business and the creation of jobs. Business success or failure is dependent upon relative performance in the free market and global economy. Businesses must offer products or services that are desired by others, customers must be willing to pay the stated price, and this dynamic must always result in the consumer believing that the value of the product or service justified the cost. But there is one more very important element that is the most critical component of the business—the generation of sustained profits. No profits, no business.

In case that didn't sink in, let's review that one more time: *no profits, no business.* No business, no jobs. No jobs, no income. No income, no tax receipts. No tax receipts, no infrastructure. No infrastructure, no trade. No trade, no free markets. No free markets, no private ownership of property. No private ownership, no freedom. No freedom, no America as we know it. Our country eventually will devolve into a government-owned and controlled replica of communist regimes where the state dictates how our labor is deployed and how the fruit of that labor is to be distributed. With our freedoms effectively annihilated, we then are forced to be led by our government like sheep down corridors to the destination of its choosing. We are letting government assume the role of determining how businesses should be managed, even though no such authority is granted them by the Constitution. We have witnessed recently the government not only dictating how businesses are to be managed, but actually *acquiring* private businesses it deemed to be "too big to fail." Such entry into the private sector, by definition, interfered with the workings of the free markets and unduly rewarded some businesses at the expense of others. The importance of competition dictating who will survive and who will falter was forever transformed when government decided to alter that dynamic. Our government has declared that it is they who will decide who wins and who loses in the business world. This undoing of the free-market forces of capitalism will eventually disrupt our economic system to such a degree that it will only lead to further business failures and further job losses. As government increases in its size and reach, individual freedoms are decreased proportionately. President Reagan said in his first inaugural address on January 20, 1981:

> "It is not my intention to do away with government. It is rather to make it work—work with us, not over us; stand by our side, not ride our back. Government can

and must provide opportunity, not smother it; foster
productivity, not stifle it.."

We would be well served as a country to embrace the same intentions.

THE DEMISE OF PERSONAL ACHIEVEMENT

I have yet to see a law emerge from Washington that mandates employees perform their jobs as required by the employer or face termination, with no right to claim undeserved compensation from taxpayers. I have yet to see a law come out of Washington that stipulates that if employees demonstrate poor performance or lack the necessary skills or abilities to perform a certain job, they have no cause of action against the employer. Yet our country would benefit immensely if such laws existed. I think one of the most illuminating examples of how the government has twisted the notion that relative skill and performance ought to be the factors that determine who gets hired, promoted, and terminated is the case of *Ricci v. DeStefano*. Doesn't ring a bell? It was the case that was noted, but not thoroughly examined, during the Supreme Court nomination process of Judge Sonia Sotomayor. While everyone was making a big to-do about her "wise Latina woman …" remarks and her videotaped statements that the judiciary does indeed make policy (even though it's unconstitutional), nobody in the media, the business community, or academia really looked at the issues surrounding this particular case. That was indeed unfortunate because it was a perfect example of how governmental intervention in the workplace has warped our sense of right and wrong and has grossly mutated the notion that personal effort and performance should be the cornerstone of job security, personal achievement, and economic prosperity. It was the perfect time to reexamine the role that government should play in the workplace, and it was the quintessential example of how overreaching laws will play a lead role in the destruction of the economic engine that produces jobs, wealth, and security for our nation.

To provide proper context, the central issues at hand in the case *Ricci v. DeStefano (07-1428 and 08-328)* revolves around a legal concept of racial discrimination called "disparate impact" discrimination. This legal doctrine of racial discrimination was put forth by the U.S. Supreme Court in a landmark case called *Griggs v. Duke Power Co.* (Griggs v. Duke Power Co., 401 U.S. 424 (1971)) Prior to the enactment of anti-discrimination laws under Title VII, Duke Power had employees allocated to five operating departments: (1) Labor, (2) Coal Handling, (3) Operations, (4) Maintenance, and (5) Laboratory and Test. Blacks were employed only in the Labor Department, where the highest paying jobs paid less than the lowest paying jobs in the other four "operating" departments, in which only whites were employed. After Title VII was enacted, it became quickly evident to Duke Power that this employment practice was clearly illegal, as it had a strong element of discrimination, or "disparate treatment," of one race over another—only whites could hold the higher paying jobs, while employees of other races could not. Therefore, there was disparate, or unequal, treatment of the races when considering which jobs would be assigned to certain employees, and because such decisions were based on an individual's race, that was a clear violation of the anti-discrimination provisions of the new law.

So, due to the fact that Duke Power had an employment policy that was in direct violation of the law, they sought to correct that by revamping its employment criteria and removing any semblance of considering race when making employment decisions. Subsequently, Duke Power instituted a new employment policy regarding which employees would qualify for certain positions. The new policy stated that in order to be considered for positions not in the Labor department, employees had to have a high school diploma and score satisfactorily on a given aptitude test. It didn't matter if you were white, black or brown, to hold certain positions required that the employee possess a high school diploma. Griggs, a black male, was denied a promotion to another job because he did not possess a high school diploma, and he filed a lawsuit under the newly enacted Title VII law. The case reached the United States Supreme Court, and the resulting decision has, to this day, significant implications on workplace decisions.

The Supreme Court took a look at the facts of this case and concluded that there was indeed discriminatory conduct that occurred, albeit subtle and seemingly unintentional. When Duke Power changed its employment criteria, the court observed that the changed policy was a noteworthy effort by Duke Power to abide by the law as it appeared that they were implementing a "race neutral" policy. However, under closer examination, the court stated that although this policy did not result in disparate, or unequal, *treatment* of employees due to race, it resulted in a disparate, or unequal, *impact* on minority candidates. The court looked not only to the selection criteria itself, but also to the end *results* of the selection methods and saw discrimination. The reasoning was that up to that point in our nation's history, minorities, and blacks more specifically, were not afforded equal access to education and were often prevented from going to school altogether. Because they did not have equal access to a high school education, there would be less black high school graduates, and therefore, there would be a statistically significant differential in the number of white high school graduates when compared to blacks. Therefore, even though Duke Power's new policy was race-neutral on its face, the effect, or *impact*, on minorities was discriminatory and therefore deemed illegal. Thus was born the disparate impact prong that would now be utilized when determining if certain actions or policies have the *effect* of discrimination, even though there was no discriminatory intent. If there appears to be a statistical discrepancy in the racial makeup of who gets selected or who gets excluded from employment, then regardless of the *intent* of the employer, it is the *result* that can also be scrutinized by the courts. And if there appears to be some disparity in the racial composition of those selected or excluded, the affected employees may bring a lawsuit against the employer for illegal discrimination.

The disparate impact theory is widely used when analyzing the effects of certain employment tests, exams, profiles, etc. If an employer uses a test to determine suitability for employment in a certain position, the test must be job-related, it must test for the relative skill level that is demanded in the actual performance of the job, and it must be a valid predictor of relative performance in that job (e.g., you can't use a chemistry test to determine someone's typing speed). If there is a statistically significant disparity in the races of those who pass or fail the test, the employer must be able to prove that the testing mechanism was valid, reliable, and predictive of performance. Absent that proof, if statistical disparities exist along racial lines between those selected and those rejected, the test can be challenged as illegal due to the disparate impact the test had on minority candidates.

It flows logically that we don't want employers using selection tests that are not relevant. But we should be focused on the accuracy and predictability of the testing mechanism itself, not the racial composition of who passed the test. Certainly, I would argue that if an employer had a test that contained one question, and the question was "Explain in your own words what it was like growing up as a middle-class white child in your community," that test would be tilted in favor of those individuals who were actually white and middle class growing up. On the other hand, let's say an employer administers a pre-employment test for applicants applying for a math teaching position. If the test question was "Multiply 5 by 12, and then divide by 3," and a statistically significant number of minorities answered incorrectly (the answer, by the way, is 20), would that test be discriminatory? I think we would all agree that the test met the criteria of being valid and predictable, and the courts would most likely view it as nondiscriminatory, in terms of it not violating the disparate treatment or disparate impact prohibitions of the law. So we have two ends of the spectrum covered here in these two examples—one that is clearly discriminatory and one that is not.

And now that takes us to Judge Sotomayor and *Ricci v. DeStefano*. The case pitted the city of New Haven, Connecticut, against approximately eighteen firefighters in that city who passed promotional exams for lieutenant and captain positions, yet were denied the promotions due to the fact that the city determined that not enough minorities passed the exam. In 2003, seventy-seven candidates completed New Haven's firefighter lieutenant exam: forty-three were white, nineteen were black, and fifteen were Hispanic. Of those, 44 percent of the candidates passed the exam: 58 percent of the white test-takers passed, 32 percent of the blacks passed, and 20 percent of the Hispanics who took the test passed. In addition, forty-one candidates took the captain exam: twenty-five were white, eight were black, and eight were Hispanic. Of those, 28 percent of the whites passed, 25 percent of the Hispanics passed, and 0 percent of the blacks passed.

The city chose to throw out the test results altogether, denied the promotions to those who passed, and decided to try another test battery that might have a less disparate impact on minorities. Notice the percentages of those who passed the tests were not that strikingly different but were viewed as statistically below the desirable pass rates for each racial category. The EEOC uses a standard called the "80 percent rule," adopted under the Uniform Guidelines on Employee Selection Procedures that provide that "a selection rate that is less than 80 percent of the rate of the group with the highest rate will generally be regarded as evidence of adverse impact." The resulting "pass/fail" statistics led to the decision to reject the results entirely. The reason behind this decision to toss out the results was that the city wanted to avoid a disparate impact discrimination charge, and instead of defend the test as legitimate, they chose to scrap everything, deny the promotions to those who passed, and look for a different test that might have "better" results, at least from a racial composition standpoint. What is quite disturbing about New Haven's decision is that they spent a considerable amount of time and money attempting to produce a nondiscriminatory test and even hired consultants to help in that effort. Yet they chose to retreat out of fear of litigation rather than stand and fight to defend the test as fair, predictable, reliable, and valid. It was a fear of lawsuits and a lack of concern for those who worked extremely hard to pass the test and prove their qualifications that turned the city of New Haven in another direction.

However, those who were denied the promotions decided they would sue the city for racial discrimination. Their argument was that the decision to throw out the test results was racially motivated and therefore a violation of Title VII. They claimed that the city engaged in clearly discriminatory conduct by denying the promotions based upon race. The district court and the appellate court (of which Sotomayor sided with the majority) ruled in favor of the city, tossing out the claim from the firefighters who passed the exam. These courts, in essence, stated that the city had the duty to toss out the results because the test did not deliver enough minorities for promotion. The case was appealed to the United States Supreme Court and on a 5–4 vote, the court reversed the lower courts (and Sotomayor) and stated that the decision to toss out the exam results was indeed race discrimination against the firefighters who passed the exam because the decision was racially motivated. The Supreme Court basically said that just because a statistically significant number of minorities failed the exam doesn't mean the exam itself it discriminatory. The Supreme Court was reluctant to arrive at the conclusion that the test itself was the problem and instead saw the test as a legitimate measure of the skills and abilities necessary to perform the duties of lieutenant or captain of the fire department. The Court ruled that throwing out the test results was discriminatory conduct as it was based upon race. The rightful conclusion by the Supreme Court, unlike the lower courts, was that a correct answer is a correct answer, regardless of the race of the person who answers it. Furthermore, it was evident that the test was not discriminatory, as six blacks and seven Hispanics passed as well. And don't overlook the fact that many white firefighters also failed the test. The case, therefore, turned into a battle of statistics versus demonstrated proficiency, as well as an overly convoluted analysis of whether an employer engaged in discrimination based upon the results of a promotional exam.

Yet the lower courts and the city of New Haven wanted to treat the minorities who passed as some sort of racial anomaly. It was as if the city, the lower courts, and the four dissenting justices on the Supreme Court were telling those six blacks and seven Hispanics that their success in passing the test could not be believed because they were minorities, and minorities could not possibly have the knowledge, dedication, skills, or abilities to pass the exam because the test was discriminatory and could not be passed by non-whites. They, in essence, determined that minorities were *predisposed* to being less capable than non-minorities in meeting the necessary standards. The message was loud and clear—if only a few minorities passed the exam compared to whites, their accomplishment was nothing more than pure luck and in no way a reflection of their efforts or abilities. I consider this to be an extremely racist point of view. They seemingly hold fast to the dangerous concept that merit, skills, abilities, knowledge, and performance don't matter—only statistics are important. Regardless of the fact that the test was carefully and painstakingly analyzed and developed to insure its validity and nondiscriminatory content, the statistical composition of those who passed took center stage, and the individuals, including blacks and Hispanics who demonstrated the requisite knowledge, skills, and abilities were denied their rightful promotions—all because there were too many non-whites who failed to pass the exam. Further, the plaintiff, Ricci, had dyslexia, which made it very difficult to study and score well on his tests, and he invested in the services of a tutor to help him prepare for the test, which he subsequently passed. But his efforts to overcome his learning disability were apparently considered inconsequential to the analysis.

This line of thinking is not only irrational; it is destructive to our workplaces. It is the same philosophy that purports that when certain individuals can't perform at the necessary performance levels, we need to lower the standards to allow low performers an opportunity to reap the same benefits earned by individuals who have worked hard and demonstrated the necessary competency. Clinging to this concept will eventually result in our workplaces being populated by individuals who are neither skilled nor knowledgeable, and hardworking employees will be displaced by the unprepared and the unwilling. Businesses will become less competitive, and jobs will continue to evaporate, but our government will take solace in the fact that the jobs that do remain will be held by incumbents who never had to prove their competency.

I have often wondered how it is that the National Basketball Association (NBA) has managed to escape charges of discrimination based upon the disparate impact theory. Black players account for approximately 79 percent of all players in the league - (Source: Journal of Sport Behavior, December 1997; by Wilbert Leonard II). There is obviously a statistical disparity in the selection rates of players entering the NBA, and one could further argue that the playing time and compensation levels for white players, on average, is much less than that of blacks. However, basketball is a game of skill, and if white players don't demonstrate that skill to the same degree as black players, should they be given any type of preferential treatment in the selection process or have their skills evaluated against a lower set of standards than black players? The answer: absolutely not. If a white player can't dribble, shoot, pass, jump, rebound, defend, or score points to the same degree as his black counterpart, then there should be no question as to who should make the team and who should get the most playing time. It's all about determining who has the requisite basketball skills that will help the team win games and championships. It doesn't really matter to the owners, coaches, and even fellow players what race someone is. All that matters is the players' skill, effort, and performance on the court. Period.

No racial overtone here, just the way it should be in basketball, or any other sport, or any other business—demonstrated skills and abilities are what should determine your ability to obtain and retain a job.

Yet our government refuses to mount their horses in pursuit of eliminating this obviously warped sense of fairness in the NBA. If we apply the same line of reasoning in the Ricci case to the NBA selection process, then we would see a completely different set of rules apply to how basketball players are selected. Once the draft and tryouts are conducted and it becomes evident that there is a statistical difference in how many white players were drafted or how many made the team, the selection process should be discarded. Maybe our government would have the NBA allow white players to be given "credit" for just hitting the rim of the basket rather than requiring the ball to actually drop through the hoop. Or maybe, after our government gets their hands on the system, we give white players three points for a basket, as opposed to only two points for black players, to offset the skill differential because, you know, white players were just not afforded the same opportunity to hone their basketball skills while growing up. Maybe, after the government levels the playing field we will have the same percentage of white players in the NBA as is reflected in general society, and the same percentage of black players as is reflected in society. Maybe we need to scrap the whole selection system for basketball players and, instead of looking at skills and ability we should instead focus on how many white players can be added to the rosters of pro basketball teams. If the same type of selection criteria and performance standards are being forced upon the business world, then maybe the sporting world needs to be held to the same standards as well.

The notion is as ridiculous as it sounds. Most anyone would, if asked, say that skill, not race, is what should determine whether someone gets selected for a sports team, and actual demonstrated performance should determine his relative compensation, playing time, and eventual release from the team. But when we put that same test to the business world, everything changes and the notion of performance-based rewards gets annihilated. Our Congress and judiciary see the business world as needing statistical balance and are seemingly unconcerned by the fact that basing employment decisions on statistics, and not merit, is inherently destructive to our economic, educational, and political systems. In the

Griggs v. Duke Power Co. case, it was a reasoned conclusion that led the courts to decide that possession of a diploma was a discriminatory selection criterion because blacks indeed were prevented from pursuing an education in many instances, and therefore such a job criteria was discriminatory. But in the Ricci case, it is unknown how the city of New Haven, and eventually the district and federal courts (and four Supreme Court justices), arrived at the conclusion that minorities were disadvantaged or somehow prevented from acquiring the necessary knowledge to pass the firefighters test. We have come a long way since Griggs, and all Americans are guaranteed access to education. All of the firemen who took the test were already employed in the firefighting profession. All of them had equal time to study, had access to the same study material, and were given the same test. They all had prior knowledge of firefighting techniques and strategies and had first-hand knowledge of the responsibilities and tasks that the lieutenants and captains had to perform when battling a fire or managing a firefighting team. So the only thing that could be discriminatory about the selection exam was that it discriminated in *favor* of those who possessed the critical skills and knowledge, and *against* those who did not.

In a way, I can't really blame the city of New Haven in the Ricci case. They decided to ditch the test results because they feared they would have been sued by those who did *not* pass, and that alone led them to decide to go in another direction so as not to have to defend the test. But, as it turns out, they were sued anyway. If they promoted the men who passed the exams, they may have been sued under the disparate impact theory of discrimination. When they decided to ditch the exam results, those who passed the test sued because the decision was based upon race, which violates the disparate treatment theory of discrimination. Just by engaging in a process of identifying promotable firemen, the city fell into a no-win situation and eventually was forced into costly litigation—all caused by our government insisting that they fully scrutinize and pass judgment on our employment decisions.

This is exactly the problem with many of our workplace laws—they force businesses into decisions that are acceptable to government but not prudent for the company. The laws require businesses to justify their actions to an attorney, a government regulatory entity, a judge, or a jury, and regardless of whether they are successful in defending their actions or decisions, they still are saddled with the exorbitant cost of paying for that defense. The city of New Haven was less concerned about the injustices against the firemen that passed the test than they were concerned about being sued and having to spend a ton of money to defend the decision. It was clearly an example of government regulations resulting in a "damned if you do, damned if you don't" dilemma that required costly litigation to sort it all out.

But I would venture to guess that most people don't care what color the firefighters are. All I know is when my house is on fire, and I have my personal possessions and loved ones in harm's way, I don't care if the lieutenant and captain are white, black, brown, or any other color or race; all I care about is whether they can manage a crisis, limit property damage, prevent casualties, and return every firefighter safely back to the station. So if the testing mechanism is such that some individuals of one race or another didn't pass the test that determines the relative ability to accomplish those things, well then so be it.

But many jurists, including Sotomayor (and the four dissenting Supreme Court justices), would have us believe that if someone can't pass such an exam, or doesn't possess the requisite knowledge to perform a job, or can't demonstrate sustained levels of acceptable performance, then it must be someone else's fault, or it must be due to something society has done to prevent the acquisition of knowledge or skill. It must be the test or the way someone was raised, but it *certainly* can't be due to the fact that someone didn't put forth the necessary effort. I find it rather ironic that Sotomayor sided with the city of New Haven in light of her accomplishment in being selected as a Supreme Court justice. As a minority and a female, she obviously had to overcome many hurdles and had to demonstrate her legal skills through hard work and a strong work ethic, which I greatly respect her for. She did not require any lowering of standards and was never evaluated against any different criteria than other lawyers and jurists. She demonstrated her proficiency the old fashion way—through hard work and sustained effort. And if she didn't perform as well on her exams in law school as other classmates, I seriously doubt she ever requested a new test be given that was "less discriminatory" Let's recall the words of Barack Obama, while addressing the United Nations in September 2009, that are printed on the first page of this book: "Nothing is easier than blaming others for our troubles and absolving ourselves of responsibility for our choices and our actions." It's much easier for the firefighters who did not pass the test to blame others for their failure when, instead, they should have taken responsibility for their choice not to properly prepare themselves for the exam.

But there are many in the judiciary and in Congress who don't see it that way and will continue to place more importance on statistics than on merit. Some judges and legislators will soon decree, "Two plus two equals four ... unless a statistically significant number of people think otherwise."

THE ASSAULT ON
BUSINESS CONTINUES

I was hoping that a new presidential administration would be a refreshing change to the politics of discord and ideology. Partisan politics had brought our political system to a standstill and nothing was being accomplished in Washington. We were promised change. We got it. I knew that the business world was in for a nightmare when the very first law that President Obama signed was the Lilly Ledbetter Fair Pay Act. Ms. Ledbetter had sued her employer for pay discrimination, alleging she was paid less than her male counterparts. But the courts told Ms. Ledbetter that her charges were untimely, as she waited too long to file her complaint. The law required those who wished to file a pay discrimination charge do so within 180 days from the date the discrimination took place. Ms. Ledbetter waited well beyond that window period and the court dismissed her case. However, not to worry—Congress would come to the rescue and change the law so that employees could sue their employer for pay discrimination without this bothersome 180-day limitation and basically make it so that every time an employee receives a paycheck, the 180-day clock for filing a charge is reset, in essence removing any time limitation on pay discrimination charges.

That change to the law is significant in that it requires employers to retain records of pay actions indefinitely because an action that took place in 1980 may not be challenged until the year 2020, based upon the allegation that the employee became aware of a potential discriminatory pay practice, not when it first happened, but forty years down the road. To require records to be retained that long, and to expect an employer to be able to prove that a pay decision was indeed not discriminatory when it occurred so long ago, is both impractical and unfair to employers. We had a law on the books that allowed for allegations of pay discrimination, but once again, Congress finds it necessary to make it easier for disgruntled employees to sue employers, even though such actions occurred decades before. And President Obama was all too eager to sign this act into law, as if there was a lack of ways in which an employee can sue their employer for wage discrimination, or whether or not it is truly advisable to allow for such expanded time frames to bring a lawsuit.

But it doesn't stop there. Let's take a closer look at some other proposed and/or enacted laws that Congress wishes to impose upon the workplace.

The Employment Non-Discrimination Act (ENDA)—this law will add sexual preference to the list of protected classes under Title VII. The legislation's primary purpose is to prohibit discrimination based upon actual *or perceived* sexual orientation or gender identity. This will include homosexuality, bisexuality, heterosexuality, and transgendered individuals. Title VII makes it unlawful to base employment actions (hiring, firing, promoting, assigning, or compensation) on someone's race, color, sex, age, national origin, religion, disability, or veteran status. The problem I have with expanding the scope of protected classes to include "sexual preference" under Title VII has little to do with my personal beliefs regarding someone's personal sexual orientation. As a matter of fact, I believe that Americans should have the right, as consenting adults, to do pretty much what they want in their own bedrooms with whomever they wish to do it (again, with another consenting adult). And this certainly needs to be allowed without the government peering into the bedroom windows. However, the right to engage in sexual behavior in the privacy of your own home is a completely different issue from having someone's sexual behaviors protected by law *in the workplace.* First, remember that all heterosexual, bisexual, and homosexual individuals are already protected under current Title VII parameters because all of those same individuals are of a certain gender, age, race, color, national origin, religion, veteran status, and disability status. Overlaying sexual preference on top of those existing protected classes is nothing more than providing a legal protection in the workplace based upon how someone engages in sexual acts. In other words, this law would protect *what we do*, which is very unlike protecting factors associated with *who we are* (e.g., race, age, gender, national origin, etc.).

Once you begin to afford legal protections for behavioral preferences, you begin that dangerous slide down the slippery slope where all behaviors are now subject to consideration of legal protections. If we are going to provide legal protections based upon individuals' sexual behaviors, we may witness calls for granting legal protections to employees who engage in hunting behaviors, or fishing, golfing, smoking, dancing, or dog fighting behaviors. We might even see calls to protect bigamists and polygamists.

I think we would all agree that most companies highly discourage employees from talking at work about their sexual exploits. And almost all companies certainly forbid engaging in sexual behaviors while at work. But this law will offer legal protections for those behaviors that occur outside of work and have absolutely nothing to do with how work is assigned, performed, or evaluated. What this administration is attempting to do is grant employees legally protected status based upon how they engage in sex. This is absolutely ludicrous and is nothing more than an attempt to give employees another avenue by which to sue their employer.

From an enforcement perspective, it presents a myriad of problematic issues associated with how to prove an employer engaged in an adverse employment action based upon someone's sexual preference. Normally, when a charge is filed under Title VII, the EEOC initiates an investigation into the allegations and asks the employer to furnish data associated with the employment action. If an employee was allegedly fired for absenteeism but claims the termination was really due to the employee's race, the EEOC will request that the employer list all of the terminations over the previous two years that were due to absenteeism and that the data be broken down by race of each of those employees terminated for that reason. The same applies to age discrimination complaints, national origin, etc. The data is then used to determine if there is a pattern of terminating employees by illegal motives.

Therefore, in almost all discrimination cases under Title VII, there is a *comparative* element in determining whether discrimination did indeed transpire. Therefore, in order to prove or disprove whether sexual preference discrimination has transpired will require the employer be made aware of the sexual preference of each employee. Take, for example, a case in which an applicant was not hired by a particular company, and the applicant alleges that the decision was based upon his sexual preference status. In order to prove that the company discriminated against this applicant, there would need to be an assumption that the employer in fact knew the applicant's sexual orientation. Secondly, there would need to be a comparative reference point, such as someone else being hired, ostensibly less qualified, who was of a different sexual orientation. But again, there would need to be an assumption that the employer knew the sexual orientations of all the applicants. Investigation of such charges will be troublesome, to say the least.

This is where the whole premise of the law falls apart. Determining if discriminatory conduct has occurred requires an analysis of how similarly situated employees are treated. For example, if an employer disciplines a black employee for absenteeism but fails to discipline a white employee who has similar attendance issues, then there could be a finding of discrimination. It's the disparate treatment prong of Title VII—treating similarly situated employees differently because of their protected class status. When you throw "sexual preference" under the Title VII umbrella, the same analysis must transpire. When an allegation is made that an employer discriminated against an employee or applicant based upon his sexual preference, there must be a basis on which to examine the conduct—namely, the relative sexual preference of each of the individuals affected by the employment action. It would appear that employers would be required to gather that data from their applicants and employees, asking them, "Do you prefer to have sex with men, women, or both?" This would appear to be an egregious violation of employees' constitutional right to privacy. Yet, the proposed law forbids the employer from asking applicants and employees their sexual preference, because that would be discriminatory. How Congress intends to enforce this law and determine whether sexual preference discrimination has occurred will be interesting. Nevertheless, I believe that close scrutiny of this ill-conceived bill will expose it as both unconstitutional and unenforceable.

Let's take this even further. If Title VII is amended to include sexual preference as a protected class, this can now open the doors to disparate *impact* claims as well. Recall the *Ricci* case where the results of a promotion exam were viewed to have a disparate impact on non-whites due to the fact that a statistically significant number of minorities failed the exam. Let's inject "sexual preference" in place of "race" and now analyze how such a scenario would be played out in the courts. The inclusion of sexual preference under Title VII would presumably allow individuals to claim that they were disproportionately excluded from promotions because the testing mechanism has a discriminatory effect on homosexuals, bisexuals or transgendered individuals. It is unknown how this would be proven or disproven unless the court has knowledge of the test-takers' sexual orientation. To make such an inquiry would seem blatantly unconstitutional. This presents a huge legal hurdle to those who find it so easy to inject sexual preference under Title VII protections because determining if discriminatory conduct occurred will require every relevant individual to *disclose* their sexual orientation.

Additionally, if sexual preference is included under Title VII protections, then *heterosexuals* could also claim discrimination. We will eventually see charges filed by disgruntled employees who claim they were discriminated against because they are straight. Again, even this allegation would require an analysis of how similarly situated employees were treated, and determine if straights were treated differently than gays, again requiring knowledge of all the affected parties' sexual preference. This is absurd and would lead to such an invasion of personal privacy that the courts would have no choice but to severely restrict how claims could be filed, how those allegations could be investigated, and how the law could be enforced.

Assume that sexual preference has been added to Title VII, and an allegation of sexual orientation discrimination has been made. Once a charge or allegation is filed, the merits of the charge must be investigated, and normally that investigation is done both internally by a company representative and also by the government agency responsible for handling the charges. Let's look at a possible scenario involving the investigation of a sexual preference discrimination complaint:

Investigator: "Hello, Ms. Jones. I am investigating an employee complaint and I will need you to provide us some information that might help us resolve the issue. Do

	you have just a moment?"
Ms. Jones:	"Sure. I will help any way I can, but I really don't have any idea why you would need to talk to me. Did I do something wrong?"
Investigator:	"Oh, no, no, not at all. You've done nothing wrong. We just have to look into some allegations that pertain to you."
Ms. Jones:	"I don't understand."
Investigator:	"Well, do you remember the promotion that you were awarded last month?"
Ms. Jones:	"Yes, of course. I was very proud of that."
Investigator:	"Yes, I'm sure you were. Well, there were other employees who were also under consideration for that promotion, and one of them has filed a complaint claiming the decision to award the job to you instead of him was illegal because the company denied him the promotion due to his sexual preference."
Ms. Jones:	"Well, that is so disheartening. Why is someone making these accusations? I feel that I was very qualified for this job and I believe I earned my promotion because of my experience and my performance and my dedication to this company."
Investigator:	"I understand. But I have to investigate these allegations and try to determine if, indeed, any employment decisions were based upon someone's sexual preference. So, I need to ask you some questions to help me get to the bottom of this."
Ms. Jones:	"Okay. I'll try to help you in any way possible."
Investigator:	"Great. Then let's proceed. The first thing I will need to know from you is … how do you have sex?"
Ms. Jones:	*"Excuse me?"*
Investigator:	"What I mean is, do you have sex only with men … or do you like to have sex only with women?"
Ms. Jones:	"What!"
Investigator:	"Or … maybe you like to have sex with both men *and* women … you know, either/or … AC-DC … maybe a little combo action?"
Ms. Jones:	*"I beg your pardon!* I find this line of questioning totally out of line and absolutely none of your business. What gives you the right to bring me in this office and ask such inappropriate and personal questions?"

Investigator: "Just relax, Ms. Jones. For the record, *Congress* has given me the right to ask these questions, so you will need to pull yourself together and answer me so I can complete my investigation. I need to see if any employment decisions were based on how people have sex ... after all, it *is* the law ..."

This scenario will not be far from reality if we include sexual preference as a protected class under Title VII. If an employee alleges that there was an adverse employment action that transpired because of his sexual orientation, how will that be proven by the plaintiff, and how will the employer disprove the allegation, especially if the employer really had no knowledge of the employee's sexual preference? Even if an employer said, "You're fired because you're gay," or if the employee can show that comments made by the employer were abusive, harassing, demeaning, degrading, and/or malicious, and the employer flat-out admitted a strong animosity toward someone who is gay, then the case needs to be tried under *existing* Title VII protections regarding sex/gender discrimination. You don't need to add sexual preference to the mix. The action by the employer would be illegal under Title VII's sex discrimination prohibition because the employer was treating that particular employee differently because of *gender* stereotypes. The legal argument would be that the employer exhibited gender bias because of his preconceived notions of how each gender *should* behave, such as men should only have sex with women, and vice versa. The adverse treatment was based upon gender; therefore, it would be considered illegal *under existing Title VII protections* against sex discrimination, because Title VII prohibits gender bias. Passage of this act is both unnecessary and overreaching. It will require a gross invasion of privacy and acts only to create another way to sue employers and another way for employees to extract money from the employer. Personal behaviors do *not* warrant legal protections in the workplace, especially sexual behaviors. I think we would all agree that we certainly need to keep the government out of our bedrooms, but just as importantly, *the government needs to keep the bedroom out of the workplace.*

Which leads me to the next problem I have with the proposed legislation by the Obama administration, called the Workplace Religious Freedom Act, which in effect would make it much harder for an employer to claim that a particular religious accommodation for an employee would place an undue hardship on the employer's business operation. Under the religion prong of Title VII, employers are required to provide reasonable accommodation to employees whenever they wish to exercise their religious beliefs. These accommodations might take the form of allowing employees not to work weekends, rearranging work schedules to accommodate religious observance, allowing them time to observe certain times of prayer during the workday, or permitting them not to abide by certain dress codes that may violate the religious tenets of their particular religion, etc. The employer may escape this duty to accommodate only if the accommodation creates an undue hardship on the business, but proving undue hardship normally is reduced to proving that such accommodation would cost significant amounts of money or significantly interferes with work production. The newly proposed legislation would make it even harder to put forth the undue hardship defense. This proposed law will require employers to accommodate pretty much any request employees make regarding their religious beliefs and will mandate that the employer assist employees in abiding by their religious doctrines.

The problem I have with the whole issue of Title VII's inclusion of religion as a protected class is not about the prohibitions against discriminating on the basis of an employee's religious affiliation, but the whole notion of the requirement to accommodate. And my problem with accommodation is not so much about the imposition it places upon the business. I believe the whole issue of requiring employers to make accommodations for religious reasons under Title VII is *unconstitutional*. I believe the heart of the matter here is whether the First Amendment of the Constitution allows our government to *enact a law* that governs the practice of religion in the workplace.

The First Amendment expressly states that "Congress shall make no laws respecting the establishment of religion, or prohibiting the free exercise thereof" along with provisions regarding free speech and the rights to assemble and to petition the government for redress of grievances. What I find ironic is that the First Amendment has been used as the basis to challenge such actions as allowing prayer in schools, protesting manger scenes and crèche displays in public places, forcing the removal of the Ten Commandments from courthouse lobbies, and

47

even claiming that the inclusion of the words "under God" in the Pledge of Allegiance is forbidden because it violates the prohibition on the government imposing religious doctrine on unwitting participants. Our courts have, on many occasions, outlawed these practices under the premise they violate the First Amendment and that such actions are akin to the "state" advocating for a certain religion or for religion in general. Many of our courts have agreed with petitioners to the court that just allowing these actions to take place in a public domain (i.e., schools, courthouses, and city property) is equal to the state establishing a religion, and thus a violation of the Constitution. It's as if the courts have stipulated that if an individual is subjected to any type of religious display, doctrine, pronouncement, prayer, or activity, then it violates the constitutional right *not* to be subjected to such activity because it poses some form of harm on individuals who don't recognize faith and religion.

If merely allowing someone to say a prayer at a high school football game violates the First Amendment because it could be deemed to be the equivalent of the "state" establishing a religion, then actually *enacting a law* that *mandates* a business owner to accommodate someone else's religious beliefs is a violation of the First Amendment as well. The inclusion of religion under Title VII is the equivalent to the "state" enacting a law that establishes a religion or could be viewed as a preference for religion. It is unjustifiable that when individuals who are offended by prayer in school can get the court to sympathize with their argument that merely *allowing* the prayer to be uttered in a public domain is the equivalent of the government establishing a religion, but when that same religiously offended individual becomes a business owner, he not only has to tolerate the prayer, but accommodate it as well. The courts have determined that merely allowing displays of religion in public places is akin to the government establishing a religion, but actually *establishing* a law that requires religious accommodations in the workplace is somehow *not* considered a violation of the Constitution. This is just plain warped logic. I just don't buy the fact that our laws treat religion as some sort of right that we wear at all times like clothing, and that right continues to survive in the employment context to such a degree that employers are *required* to make reasonable attempts to accommodate individuals' religious practices, but as soon as we step into a public domain, that right is stripped off our backs and we are no longer afforded any accommodations for those same religious beliefs.

The issue, therefore, is not public versus private expression of religion. The issue is the government's assertion that it is constitutionally *prohibited from accommodating* religion in one area of society, but it is allowed to enact a law that *forces accommodation* of religion in another sector of society. Either government is constitutionally prohibited from enacting a law regarding the establishment of religion or it isn't. The Constitution clearly does *not* say that Congress is prohibited from enacting laws with respect to religion, unless it applies to business owners.

Under the religious protections of Title VII, "religion" has been held by the courts to mean "closely held beliefs." There is no requirement that religion is "mainstream" or that is has published doctrine, or even that it has a defined church. It means simply that a closely held belief includes whatever someone deems to be a religious doctrine, including an adherence to no religion, no deity, or no higher power whatsoever. Employers must still make reasonable accommodation for employees' religious practices, unless such accommodation would result in an undue hardship on the business.

In the 2009 case *EEOC v. Papin Enterprises, Inc.* (No. 6:07-CV-1548, MDL FL, 2009) the EEOC filed suit on behalf of an employee who claimed that her religion required her to wear a nose ring at all times. The female claimant worked in a Subway restaurant as a sandwich maker, and the manager requested that she remove her nose ring while working the sandwich line, as it violated their dress code and could be a violation of food safety standards and potentially damaging to the restaurant's "public image." She refused to remove the ring, claiming it violated her religious convictions. She produced no evidence of a specific religion, was unable to submit any authoritative written text pertaining to any stated beliefs of this so-called religion, and offered nothing in terms of putting forth the names or identities of any religious leaders that required the wearing of the nose ring. She merely stated that her "religion" required her to wear a nose ring at all times. The restaurant offered to allow her to wear a bandage over the ring, as well as some other accommodations, but none were accepted by the employee, and she was subsequently fired. She then filed a charge with the EEOC, and they proceeded to take up her cause in order to protect her right to wear a nose ring at work, under the banner of religious discrimination and failure to properly accommodate. They required no proof that a "religion" even existed; they just needed to hear her stipulate that perpetual nose ring wearing was a closely held religious belief.

This is what we are spending our tax dollars on. This is the type of nonsense that causes businesses to spend tens of thousands of dollars on defending their actions to government regulators and plaintiffs' attorneys. In reality, what this business owner was really attempting to do was run his business as he saw fit and that best contributed to its chance of success. Regardless of the business owners' "closely held belief" that their employees shouldn't wear facial jewelry that may be considered repugnant by their patrons or considered a violation of the dress code, our legal system chooses instead to protect the nose ring-wearing individuals who claim they will have their religious beliefs trammeled upon if they are required to remove the piece of jewelry while at work. Yet our Congress, our courts, and our regulatory agencies don't seem to grasp how these mandates are significantly countervailing to the efficient operation of the business. Employers are forced into accommodating every whim and demand of the employee, including the obligation to accommodate closely held beliefs that prove to be dubious at best, even if they contradict any of the closely held beliefs of the business owner.

Therefore, as a Christian, if I am a business owner and one of my employees is a Satanist and requests accommodations to practice his satanic beliefs, I am required to do so if it imposes no undue hardship on my business. It doesn't matter that my beliefs are completely opposed to the worshipping of Satan—the government says I must provide reasonable accommodation. The same holds true for the Jewish business owner who must accommodate a Muslim's religious practices, or a Muslim business owner who must accommodate the religious beliefs of a Jew. There is no provision under Title VII that says that reasonable accommodation is unnecessary if such actions conflict with the business owner's religious belief. Yet by requiring the business owner's religious beliefs to have no bearing on the duty to accommodate, the government is favoring one religion (the employee's) over someone else's (the business owner's). Therefore, Congress has indeed *made a law respecting the establishment of religion* (Title VII and the requirement to reasonably accommodate) and has *prohibited the free exercise thereof* (preventing the business owner from abiding by his own religious tenets). But it seems that Congress and the courts wish to ignore this fact and choose to *prohibit* accommodations for prayer at school but have no problem with establishing laws that *require* accommodations for prayer in the workplace. The hypocrisy is overwhelming.

It is my assertion that inclusion of "religion" in Title VII is clearly unconstitutional due to a violation of the First Amendment. Further, similar to "sexual preference," religion is a *behavior* as well. It is a choice that we all make to either follow a certain religion or reject religion altogether. It is not a trait we are born with, and our adherence to any particular religion can change. Therefore, any *behavioral* aspect of a person's life should fall outside of the purview of Title VII. I do feel that businesses should attempt to work with employees and try to accommodate their requests whenever possible, but there should be a line drawn between working with an employee and *requiring* accommodation.

Maybe we should require the *employee* to accommodate the employer. There needs to be an emphasis on the fact that the employer is the one who is providing the job, the paycheck, the benefits, and the way of life for the employee, and therefore, the wishes of the *employer* should take precedent regarding matters of the business. Under current law, the business owner is forced to compromise his business operations in order to accommodate the individual who says he can't work on Saturday, or needs to have prayer time facing the wall closest to Jupiter at 2:00 PM, or is required to wear a giant nose ring because it's her "closely held belief." But there is no similar requirement on employees to accommodate the employer by altering their religious practices, just a bit, so that they can perform the responsibilities of their job. If such a compromise is not allowed by their closely held belief, then the employee should have to make the choice of whether to stay employed in that particular job or seek alternative employment. It should not be the business owner's responsibility to make sure everyone has their work schedules or responsibilities modified to appease the employees' religious beliefs. It is the employee who needs to determine if those beliefs can still be followed while performing the required responsibilities of the job, or find another employer who will.

Once again, with just a little bit of fairness and common sense by Congress, and with just a bit of deference to the business community, we might have seen a law that attempts to take into consideration the religious beliefs of all parties concerned, as well as the need for continuity of business operations. If Congress had even an inkling of concern for the business owner, the law would state:

> *Employers may not refuse to hire an employee solely because of his religious affiliation or beliefs. At the time an offer of employment is made, employers are required to indicate the compensation level for the position, expected working hours, normal weekly schedules, job responsibilities, dress codes, and other factors of the job that are significant when considering acceptance or rejection of said offer. However, upon acceptance of an offer of employment and upon commencement of work, employees are required to perform the job as directed and to work the required schedules put forth by the employer. Employers are encouraged to consider employees' requests for schedule or job modifications that may interfere with their religious beliefs. However, such modifications or changes are at the sole discretion of the employer, and if the employer does not abide by such requests, the employee has no cause of action against that employer, except to resign his employment …*

But, I doubt Congress views this type of compromise as acceptable, and will continue to press their agenda for more regulatory controls over the workplace. For further proof, read on.

The Employee Free Choice Act (EFCA)—this proposed law will drastically change the landscape of labor and management relations, specifically changing the whole balance of protections contained in the National Labor Relations Act (NLRA). Under the NLRA, union and management are both prohibited from engaging in certain unfair labor practices and are required to follow certain rules regarding the union organizing campaigns. The NLRA has been on the books for over seventy years and is what I consider to be a shining example of a piece of legislation that goes to great lengths to provide rights and protections for both employees and employers. It has served the labor relations process extremely well over the years and has been the cornerstone of governance over issues related to union elections, collective bargaining, contract administration, grievance handling, and arbitration. The law was strongly supported by the unions and employees as a mechanism to secure workers rights to join together and collectively bargain over wages, hours, terms, and conditions of employment. The labor relations process even has its own system of enforcement and conflict resolution through the establishment of the National Labor Relation Board (NLRB) to insure fair labor practices and to rule on violations of the law. Politics often clouds the impartiality the NLRB is supposed to exhibit, but for the most part, the pendulum has swung in fairly close proximity to the middle ground between the rights of labor and that of management.

Under current law, when a union wishes to organize a certain company, they talk to the company's employees and attempt to convince them that they would be better served by being represented by a union. The union then attempts to obtain signed "union authorization cards" from as many employees as possible (often referred to as "card checks"), which they can then present to management as proof that the employees wish to be represented by a union. If the union obtains at least 30 percent of the designated bargaining unit, they can petition the NLRB to hold a secret ballot election to allow employees to voice their true desires, outside of any intimidation techniques by the union or the company.

You see, it's quite easy for a union to get authorization cards signed because they are nonbinding, and employees often sign them just to appease the union rep standing there requesting the signature. The NLRB and the courts have repeatedly determined that the secret ballot election is the best and fairest mechanism to determine the desires of the employee populace. It allows employees to cast a secret ballot, not viewable by union bosses or management representatives, and insures anonymity and confidentiality of the individual's vote so that the employee will not be subjected to harassment, threats, intimidation, and/or coercion. It is a system that is fair and designed to protect the privacy interests of each individual employee.

However, over the course of the last twenty-five years, unions have been losing membership at a significant rate. According to the Bureau of Labor Statistics, the union membership rate in 1983 was 20.1 percent.

In 2008, union members accounted for 12.4 percent of wage and salary workers. Union workers declined by 1.6 million from 1983 to 2008. (Source: Bureau of Labor Statistics; Economic News Release, January 28, 2009) The reasons for the declining numbers are many and varied. One reason is that union jobs began to be shipped to foreign locations due to the escalation of wages and labor costs in union environments. This resulted in many businesses not being able to compete in the new global marketplace, and it led to the transfer of many jobs to other parts of the globe where labor costs were lower and more in line with their competitors. This, in turn, began to change how some employees viewed the role of unions, and they began to question whether their tactics were really serving their best interests or were actually counterproductive to business success and job security. Additionally, there has been a declining need for unions due to the proliferation of employment laws that grant privileges, benefits, and protections to employees, regardless of whether they are represented by a union or not.

So, as unions watch their membership numbers shrink further and further, they experience a significant drop in the money collected from union dues to finance their operations and power structure. Desperation is sinking in and they have turned to Congress for their survival. Thus enters the aforementioned Employee Free Choice Act, which is blatantly designed to shift the balance of power heavily toward unions and away from management by allowing a complete revision of the secret ballot election process. It is quite ironic that the proposed law is named the Employee Free Choice Act because, in reality, it actually *destroys* the secret ballot election process and *eliminates* employees' free choice completely.

Under this bill, if the union obtains singed authorization cards from 50 percent (plus one) of the bargaining unit, the secret ballot election is eliminated altogether, and the union is automatically granted representation status over the employees. No secret ballot, no opportunity to confidentially cast your vote as to whether you want a union to represent you, no restrictions on the means or methods of obtaining the authorization cards, no prohibitions on intimidation tactics used to get employees to sign such cards, and no restrictions or prohibitions on publishing names of employees who refused to sign such cards. Therefore, unions, and many congressional supporters of unions, wish to advocate non-democratic means as the preferred method to force union representation upon employees and businesses. They wish to take away the most fundamental right we have as Americans: the right to cast a secret ballot for whichever candidate or proposition that aligns with our personally held convictions.

I can't help but wonder what it is about the secret ballot vote that troubles unions so much. It might be they are afraid that employees will vote against being represented by a third party that collects money to fight their battles, only to see them engage in tactics that raise the cost of doing business to such a degree that they are actually *less* job secure than if there was no union at all. It might be that they fear that employees will see how unions protect poor performers with the same fervor that they protect strong performers, which contributes to their employer being less competitive and, therefore, less able to keep all employees employed. Or maybe unions want employees to embrace the idea that there is no limit to how much money employers can spend on wages and benefits. Maybe they wish to perpetuate the preposterous notion that if employees had union representation, wages and benefit costs suddenly become insignificant and job security can be guaranteed without end. Maybe unions want to pass EFCA because they feel that employees are just too ignorant to make wise and reasoned decisions about their need for third-party representation. It may be all of those, but it is most likely because unions know their tactics are outmoded, their presence in business has led to their own demise, and they are so desperate to cling to the power they still have that they will do anything, even deny employees their right to a secret ballot to improve their chances of getting new dues-paying members. Unions do not have employees' best interest at heart; they have their own survivability at stake. The employees' right to secret ballot elections is creating barriers for unions to represent more workers, and unions will obtain a distinct advantage through this legislation. And this administration is clearing the way for that to happen.

Unions want to insure a continued flow of union dues to pay for their own power structure, their own political agenda, and their own organizing drives to add more members to their rolls. What employees don't seem to grasp is that unions *are* a business, just like the employer that pays their wages, and the services they provide are third-party negotiations of employment terms and conditions. They charge money to do that, and the employees pay for that service. When the employees' company is unable to compete because of the burdens of high labor costs and unions' restrictive practices related to manpower utilization, and employees are laid off because of those conditions, do you think the national union leaders are laid off as well? The answer is: absolutely not. Union bosses are not subject to the terms of the collective bargaining agreement and their employment is not affected by strikes, lockouts, or the collapse of the business. Further, union committeemen, stewards, and officers who are the local representatives at the employer's location negotiate "super seniority" clauses into the contract, protecting them from layoffs. Super seniority places the union representative at the very top of the seniority list where he can never be impacted by business downturns and subsequent layoffs. If an employer is forced to reduce the number of employees because the cost of doing business has risen so significantly due to the presence of a union, I can assure you, those who were responsible for negotiating the contract terms will not be found on the unemployment line or seeking food stamps.

Let there be no mistake—unions significantly increase the cost of doing business. I have negotiated, or been involved in the negotiation, of several collective bargaining agreements, and have studied many others. When looking at how wage levels are determined, every single one of those union contracts had pay rates determined solely by job classification. Not a single contract allowed any differences in pay to be based upon how employees actually perform the assigned duties. The company was not allowed to pay higher wages to the best performers and lower wages to poor performers; all employees in that classification had to be paid the same. Further, those same employees were strictly limited in the duties they could perform, and if the employer attempted to assign any work that was outside the scope of that classification, the employee could rightfully refuse to perform those tasks. And when the company experienced economic downturns that required layoffs and other adjustments to manpower levels, those layoffs had to be conducted solely on the basis of seniority and not on demonstrated performance, skill level or versatility of each employee. Such restrictions on the employer only act to raise labor costs, decrease efficiencies, and destroy the ability of a company to assign work to the most qualified and best performing employees. And unions accomplish all of this with the threat of a strike if the company fails to meet their demands.

I find it ironic that during the financial markets meltdown, President Obama was admonishing the bank executives for their lucrative compensation packages, and he proposed that a new system needed to be implemented that insured "pay for performance" so that the banks that performed poorly would not unduly reward those who were responsible for unacceptable results. So, the President feels it is appropriate to implement pay for performance systems in banks, but not in union environments. He finds it desirable to tie pay levels of executives to the actual value they add, but at the same time, supports unions that force businesses to pay by job title, not performance, and require protection based upon seniority, not contributions. Pay for performance should be the compensation system of choice for bank executives; but pay for performance is just as effective and necessary for all other employees too, regardless of any union affiliation. When businesses are saddled with the pay practices and employee management systems that unions advocate, they will struggle to remain competitive in the long run.

All you need for an example is to look at the situation at General Motors. GM has gone bankrupt mainly because of two things: poor management decisions and failed labor tactics—the perfect one-two punch that will lead to the demise of any organization. GM management was remarkably naive and stubborn in their inability to recognize and concede that their market share was being eroded by competition from the Japanese who were out-engineering them, out-designing them, out-marketing them, and had a more sensitive finger on the pulse of the buying public. Yet GM maintained its massive bureaucracies, unnecessary management levels, and slow-to-react development systems. Those failings allowed foreign competition to do the following: introduce higher-quality vehicles that the public demanded, offered more appealing designs, and produced models that met the consumers' needs. All the while, the unions in America were demanding higher and higher wages and more lucrative benefit and retirement plans, while at the same time offering GM nothing in regard to allowing them to become more efficient by streamlining manufacturing processes that utilize less labor. Jobs needed to be protected, the unions claimed, while they engaged in strike and work stoppages to force their agenda. Well, look at all those jobs they protected. Thousands are gone because the work systems that labor and management were building were nothing more than a house of cards bound to collapse under its own weight of high labor cost, inefficient operations, and incompetent management. It is a business model for failure. But President Obama and Congress want to perpetuate this model and force it upon the rest of American businesses. Political paybacks are taking precedent over sound legislative and economic policy.

By increasing the spread of unions throughout our business landscape, we will be increasing the cost of doing business, decreasing the efficiency and effectiveness of doing business, and causing more and more companies to suffer economic loss resulting in further job erosion. Yet the president and Congress think that's exactly what our country needs—more unions, higher cost of doing business, and inevitable job loss, all occurring during some of the worst economic conditions our nation has faced. If this law passes, I feel our nation will suffer irreversible damage. Passage of this law will highlight just how ignorant and shortsighted our politicians have become. It will be further proof that Congress and the White House care nothing about our economic survival and will stop at nothing to return political favors, even when it results in our inability to compete in the global economy, forces businesses to close or relocate, and continues to destroy jobs. Their support of this bill is indefensible.

If employees wish to organize, so be it. They should and do enjoy that right already. There is no lack of opportunity for unions to organize any business it deems ripe for representation. But employees are the ones who need to make that ultimate decision, free from intimidation or coercion from either labor or management, and our *current* laws guarantee that right to employees. EFCA will only tilt the delicate balance that is woven into the NLRA in favor of unions, while at the same time actually diminishing the right of employees to a truly "free choice" in the matter. But you can still hear the unions claim that by eliminating the right to a secret ballot election, it is actually providing them a free choice. That should speak volumes to those employees who are considering allowing a union to fight their battles for them.

However, I will still offer a recommendation to unions to spur their growth as well. You see, I'm not advocating that we outlaw unions or forbid them from attempting to organize workers. I believe unions should be a part of the business landscape because I think they perform a very important function—they serve as a constant reminder to business owners of what can happen to their business if they treat employees poorly, abusively, and/or undeservedly. When businesses view their employees from the perspective that they are unimportant, then employees and their unions will view businesses from the perspective that the company's bottom line is unimportant as well. Therefore, it is critical that management and non-management understand that they are dependent upon each other to survive. Without employees, there is no business. Without a business, there are no jobs. The more successful the business, the more secure the jobs. And, as examined earlier, when there is an abundance of highly talented employees, this cycle just perpetuates itself and the business and the employees are more secure. However, when you throw in the poorly performing employee into this system, it begins its decent into inefficiency, ineffectiveness, and unprofitability, hurting both the business and the employees.

Therefore, both management and non-management need to be pulling in the same direction to insure each other's existence. Labor and management relations must be collaborative, not combative. Failing to understand this dynamic is exactly where unions have lost their way. They want to fight their battles the way their genetic makeup forces them to, which is to keep the process adversarial. So listen up, unions. I have the answer to your waning popularity, your declining membership numbers (and dues), and your inability to ever *truly* guarantee anyone's continued employment. If you adopt my recommendations, I honestly believe you can drastically increase your membership and your revenue, and significantly raise the standard of living for every single one of your members. But it will require you to commit to some major life changes.

First, you must stop protecting poor performers. You are cutting your own throat. From my experience, I have come to the following conclusion: In a typical union shop, about 70 percent of the union workers are paid competitively and are compensated at a level that properly reflects the work they perform and the manner in which they perform it. I would also say that about 10 percent of the workers are *underpaid*, meaning had it not been for the fact that the wage rates for their particular job or classification are collectively bargained and ultimately determined by the contract, their contributions nonetheless are really of a *higher* value than reflected in their pay rate. They possess a certain set of skills and abilities that go beyond the average, and their work ethic makes them some of the best and most appreciated employees in the business. But the business is kept from paying those high performers more lucratively than their counterparts, because the union contract forbids that. Finally, that leaves the rest of the bargaining unit, which is the remaining 20 percent—or otherwise known as the *bottom 20 percent.* This is the group that is paid much *more* than they are worth. They are the employees who receive wages that are nowhere near commensurate with the value of their contributions. These are the employees who are adding significant cost, not value, to the organization through their errors, their scrap rates, their lack of effort, their unproductiveness, their absenteeism, and their proclivity to file meritless grievances, charges, and lawsuits. These are the employees who cause businesses to lose their competitive advantages and cause many to fail. Yet, unions have no problem sharing the spoils of negotiations with that 20 percent that were actually earned by the other 80 percent. If you believe my statistics (which are totally unscientific), from a compensation standpoint, 20 percent of the bargaining unit is much better off due to the presence of a union because they get more pay and job protection than they deserve. Conversely then, 80 percent of the employees are either no better off *or are worse off* because of the union's presence in the picture. Twenty percent are better off; 80 percent are not. This method of rewards distribution is not in the best interest of most employees.

The fact of the matter is, unions cannot continue to seek higher pay and better benefits for their members *while at the same time* protect poor performers, limit how the company can utilize labor, and prevent headcount adjustments from being based upon the relative contributions employees make to the company. They can't continue to increase the cost of labor without allowing the business the ability to implement the best labor strategies that can cover those increased costs. They will kill the business and kill their own jobs. Wake up unions. Take a basic economics class. When revenue can no longer cover the cost of doing business, then wages and benefits get slashed, jobs get eliminated, and/or the business fails. If you want higher pay, better benefits, and increased job security, then get smart and quit biting the hand that feeds you. Take a new approach. Re-engineer yourself.

First, you approach the business and offer a new deal. Tell management that you will allow them to freely hire and fire whomever they feel is necessary and agree to let the business utilize that labor however it deems fit so as to become the most efficient, effective, and profitable company in their market. Next, have the business establish a baseline number of employees that are necessary to support any given sales volume. If the business stipulates they need two hundred employees to support ten million dollars in sales volume, hold them to those numbers. Then, require the business to retain that number of employees as long as those sales volumes are met. This is where you obtain a measure of job security, a guaranteed number of jobs for any given sales volume. Finally, and most importantly, require a certain percentage of the profits that those sales volumes produce to be shared with the bargaining unit employees. Negotiate these terms under a collective bargaining agreement, and fight for generous profit-sharing levels, competitive time-off policies, good benefits, and a safe work environment. Seniority plays a role, but it is reserved for determining vacation levels, benefit co-pays, and as a tiebreaker for making employment decisions when "all other things are equal." The business can now actually consider these demands and agree to their inclusion in the contract because the profit levels can now sustain the cost of providing these fringes.

This arrangement gets both the union members and the business working for a common cause: higher margins. This allows for the business and the union members to obtain bigger financial rewards and enjoy increased job security. The more profits that are generated, the more money is shared among all the players, and when profits are healthy, job security is significantly enhanced. This also gets *all* of the employees working together to increase those margins because they have a vested interest in the outcome. It also aligns all the parties in a common perspective. Everyone sees how ineffective employees have a corresponding negative effect on the bottom line and, eventually, the wallets of all involved. The more the company is riddled with poor performers, slackers, and non-contributors, the less efficient and profitable the company becomes, resulting in less profit sharing and less guaranteed jobs. This results in the whole workforce taking a vested interest in who gets hired and who gets retained. Everyone now becomes concerned with recruiting employees who can make significant contributions, and everyone becomes concerned when employees stop pulling their weight. Co-workers start prodding the lazy to shape up because slackers harm everyone, and their continued presence puts more burdens on the rest of the organization. Non-contributors are cost drivers, and escalating costs cut into profit sharing and job security for the rest of the team. And it *is* a team in this environment—everyone pulling for a common cause, all striving to be as efficient and effective as possible, all obtaining enhanced rewards for improved results. But remember, the deal is that the employer maintains the absolute unencumbered right to hire and fire his employees as necessary to satisfy the needs of the business, and such decisions hinge on the relative skills, abilities, and performance of the employee.

However, I am quite certain that will be the sticking point for the unions and they just won't be able to agree to such an arrangement. Instead, they will fall back on old tactics, worn-out negotiating techniques, self-destructive practices, and job-killing legislative proposals. So my recommendation to union members is to take a good long look at who your union leaders are ostensibly "protecting." Collective bargaining tactics of old are resulting in increased cost structures that businesses simply cannot sustain in the long run. Unions need to understand basic economics: Revenue − Cost = Profit

If you drive up costs to the point that they exceed revenue, *everyone loses*. So if unions want new life, want new members to join their cause, and desire increased prosperity for all, then *protect the performers*. Fight for *them*. They are the ones who truly deserve the recognition, the compensation, the benefits, the retirement packages, and the job security. Align with the common interests of those who have the biggest stake in the game—the employer and the employee. Develop what I would refer to as "performance-based unions" where the employer and the employees hold each other accountable for each other's success and share in the fruits of that labor. If unions want to truly stimulate a growth in union membership, they need to embrace this approach. I know there are millions of highly talented employees who would love for their true worth and value to their company to be recognized and rewarded accordingly, but because of a lack of collective action, they cannot bear enough pressure on the employer to consider a different method of rewards distribution. Represent them, and unions will fill their stable with the champion racers, the winners, the ones that breed success. They are the ones who really carry the clout in the workplace, because they are the ones who produce value and profits. They are like the star athlete who is constantly sought after by all the teams because of the difference that athlete makes on an organization. And what happens to the salaries of those athletes who have proven their worth? I think we all know the answer to that. The successful, the talented, and the dependable—they make the most money because they contribute the most. Unions should take on the role of talent agents whose role is to secure the best deals for the highest performers. There are many companies that have star performers who are not compensated according to their contributions, and that is a situation that should be rectified. Businesses need to pony up more money to the highest performers, and therein exists a tremendous opportunity to exert some leverage to obtain higher wages for the superstars. However, unions wish to fight for higher wages and better benefits for *every* employee, regardless of contribution, and in spite of the fact that underperformers are responsible for dragging down the ability of the rest of the employees to have more lucrative compensation packages, better benefits, and more job security.

The labor movement's insistence on clinging to the philosophy that jobs should be protected based on seniority instead of performance, and its unwillingness to allow the employer to utilize the human talent element in the most effective manner, dooms its existence and will forever keep the highly talented performers from embracing its message. Change the approach, and unions may even get businesses to open up to the idea that they are not there to harm them, but are there to fight for the cause of the deserving. It would make for much less contentious organizing campaigns and may even be a model of doing business that is actually accepted by the business community. Businesses might realize it forces them to be better managers of human capital, which leads to increased profits, better paid workers, higher morale, and shared sacrifice.

Unfortunately, I'm quite certain they will not change their colors and will continue to engage in the destructive methods of the past that are proven losers. They will turn to government to help fight their battles. They will insist that employees be stripped of their right to vote on whether or not they want unions to be involved in their workplace issues. They will adhere to the old ways of making threats to strike if demands are not met, and they will continue to protect the employees who force others to carry their load. Unions will get certain politicians to attempt to convince the whole country that this is really the way to promote economic stability and insure a growing middle class. But I guess it is consistent with their overall strategy of providing protections for the undeserving, mandating pay and benefit levels that are out of step with contribution and effort, restricting the contributions of the high performers, creating business and job instability, and making sure that government is the leading force in making it happen. It has been occurring for some time, but never to the degree that is happening now.

Laws such as the ones mentioned above are just a few of the laws currently pending in Congress. Their passage is likely unless America wakes up and takes up the cause to stop these job-killing pieces of … legislation. But, as we can see, Congress and the courts have been contributing to job killing for decades with their continual encroachment on the workplace. And it's no coincidence that unemployment rates are at their highest level in over thirty years. Politicians condemn corporate executives who have taken their businesses overseas in an effort to better compete against foreign competition, but fail to see that the competition overseas enjoy lower labor costs, less government intrusion, and readily available workers who have not been raised with the entitlement mentality we have created here in the United States. Many proclaim that such strategies are nothing more than modern-day exploitation of third-world labor markets. It is a dilemma that I too have struggled with. Some of my past employers had manufacturing operations in foreign countries where the labor rates were significantly cheaper. Even though the working conditions were exceptional and the plants themselves were clean, well lit, and air-conditioned, the wage rates amounted to approximately 50 cents per hour, as compared to the U.S. minimum wage of $5.35 per hour (at that time). Some of my friends and relatives would ask, "How can you take advantage of those people in that way?" My answer was that without our presence, those people had no way of making a living. Without the U.S. companies that employed them, there would be no jobs, no wages, and no standard of living. The employees themselves were very appreciative of our presence. They wanted us to be there. They wanted us to stay and bring even more jobs for their family members. The fact that the labor rates were much lower than what was paid in the United States was really inconsequential to them. They needed the jobs and we provided them. It allowed those individuals to pay for food, clothing, and shelter. It stimulated the local economies as more people paid, bartered, and traded for goods and services. It also allowed us to remain competitive in our market where we were competing against both domestic and foreign companies that had access to global labor markets as well. This, in turn, allowed us to keep significantly more of our employees working and competitively paid. Therefore, the net effect of lowering our overall labor costs was the ability to keep more individuals employed in the United States and in our foreign locations. That is not worker exploitation; it is the realities of global markets and worldwide competition.

But our government keeps attempting to restrain businesses from competing in the global market through legislative mandates, and because of it, our economy is losing jobs by the millions. As businesses become saddled with more and more costs associated with government intrusions in the workplace, they are less able to retain earnings, create jobs, distribute rewards to employees, and grow the enterprise. As jobs are cut, laid-off individuals are laying claim to unemployment benefits in unprecedented numbers. This has led to the depletion of available unemployment funding for the millions of unemployed. Our governmental officials respond to this crisis with a requirement that unemployment benefits be extended and increased, which, by the way, are completely funded by business taxes. The government's solution to this problem is to raise taxes on businesses to fund the unemployment programs. The unemployment system is being inundated by newly terminated employees who have lost their jobs because of the financial collapse of our economy, much of which the government helped create with their irresponsible policies. We are experiencing no true economic expansion. No amount of stimulus money directed to our unemployment funds will solve the root cause of the problem, and further increases in payroll taxes will only exacerbate it. The nation's unemployment system is the quintessential example of all that is wrong about our workplace regulations.

The only way we can solve the unemployment crisis is to understand the only way it can be solved—with the creation of jobs. You cannot solve this issue with government unemployment extensions or higher taxes. All of those "fixes" are temporary at best and counterproductive at worst. Unemployment is *the* most significant factor preventing economic recovery. Unless we have job creation, there can be no absorbing of the unemployed back into the workforce. So how can we "stimulate" job creation? Let me offer a viable solution.

THE UNEMPLOYMENT SOLUTION

The unemployment insurance (UI) system is administered at the state level but overseen by the federal government. Unbeknownst to most people, in almost every state in the nation, unemployment benefits are funded solely by employers. That's right. Businesses fund the unemployment system—not employees, not the government, not the taxpayers. This is accomplished thorough the imposition of taxes called SUTA (State Unemployment Tax Act) and FUTA (Federal Unemployment Tax Act). These taxes are paid by the employer as a percentage of their total payroll dollars, up to a certain maximum. These taxes are then paid to the state and federal government to be used to pay unemployment benefits to employees who have lost their jobs, and to pay for the states to administer these benefits, process claims, etc. In most states, the tax rate that the employer is required to pay to fund these benefits is based upon how many unemployment claims are filed by their ex-employees. Normally, that tax rate is derived by calculating a ratio of the amount of claims dollars paid to claimants, against the total dollar amount of the payroll. So, in cases where an employer is reducing payroll (e.g., layoffs, job eliminations, etc), and employees file for unemployment benefits, that ratio is adversely affected because payroll dollars are reduced and unemployment claims increase. The result is further tax increases to keep the UI system properly funded. In times of economic downturn, like we are experiencing now, commerce and trade decline, businesses lose profits, payrolls begin to be slashed through job elimination and layoffs, and unemployment claims rise significantly.

Unemployment funds in many states are now bankrupt, and each and every week, more and more states will soon experience a similar fate. With the continued expansion of unemployment benefits, both in dollars and duration, the current system will eventually be unsustainable. As businesses continue to take drastic actions to shed costs in order to survive the economic downturn, employment levels will continue to drop and unemployment levels will continue to rise. As payrolls continue to shrink, there is a corresponding reduction in payroll taxes paid to sustain the unemployment funds. To help shore up the depleted coffers of unemployment funding, the current system requires that SUTA taxes be increased and assessed to businesses. In light of the current expansions of benefits brought on by both the economic conditions of the United States and the subsequent "stimulus bill" that mandated these expansions, tax increases will have to be significant and ongoing. Such significant tax increases result in even further burdens on businesses, and most will respond accordingly with continued job cuts. These actions will, in turn, increase the number of individuals applying for unemployment benefits, further depleting the available funds, thus requiring additional tax increases, and so on. And as this vicious cycle continues to spin out of control, the financial solvency of the UI system is destroyed and it eventually collapses. Congress responds with tax increases and benefit extensions. Even more astonishing, Congress has also proposed that eligibility for UI benefits be *broadened* so that even individuals who would normally be disqualified from benefits can now obtain unemployment payments. As part of the stimulus bill and subsequent legislation, unemployment benefits have been extended for up to ninety-three weeks, or longer under certain conditions. Because many of the state unemployment funds are bankrupt, the federal government is providing loans to these states so that they can continue to pay unemployment benefits, but in return for these loans, states are forced to enact two of the following four benefit expansions in order to qualify for federal funds:

1. Pay unemployment benefits to individuals seeking only part-time work.
2. Extend unemployment benefits to workers in training after they have exhausted regular UI benefits.
3. Allow employees to receive UI benefits after they have quit their jobs because of "compelling family reasons," such as

domestic abuse, caring for ill family members, or following a spouse who has accepted employment that will require relocation.

4. Increase the UI benefit amount by a minimum of fifteen dollars for every dependent of an unemployed individual.

Therefore, Congress feels that to solve the unemployment funding crisis, we must extend UI eligibility for almost two years and also change the laws to allow people *to quit their current jobs* because of personal reasons. This is not prudent policy. Now is not the time to be changing the regulations so that *more* employees can *voluntarily* leave jobs to go on unemployment, especially in light of the fact that our unemployment funds are going bankrupt each day. Their logic is almost laughable if it weren't so warped and dangerous. Employees should not be eligible for unemployment when they quit their job because their spouse obtained employment elsewhere that requires relocation. Such decisions are personal ones, and employers should not have to fund unemployment benefits for employees who voluntarily leave their jobs. Further, when employees quit for compelling family reasons, the determination of what constitutes a "compelling reason" will apparently be evaluated by government employees, not the employer. There is also no guidance as to what a legitimate "family illness" is, and no mention of who will make that determination. We do not know how the existence of such medical conditions will be proven, and to whom it needs to be proven to. Even if we wish to open a national debate as to whether these situations *should* allow for unemployment eligibility, it is nothing short of negligent to include these provisions while we are in the midst of one of the worst economic crises this nation has endured. But right on cue, Congress wants to offer up benefits that we can't afford to pay, to individuals who should not be allowed to receive them, creating more incentives not to work, during a time when job creation should be our highest priority.

The cost of funding these enhancements will fall squarely on the backs of businesses. Taxes will have to be increased *significantly* to cover these additional costs. This will result in further burdens on the businesses to cover these additional expenses, and in many cases, it will necessitate additional employment reductions. Congress has perfected the system of taxing businesses, enacting laws that allow only them to control how that tax money is spent, and then taking credit for looking after the downtrodden. Yet these policies will do nothing but *create* more unemployment and further entrench this country into economic recession. The actions by Congress and this administration will only stifle job growth and economic prosperity for both businesses and affected individuals. It's as if government *wants* people to be unemployed and dependent upon them for entitlements, and they are creating a system that encourages them to remain out of work. This approach is destined for complete failure and will do nothing but further delay any economic recovery. The time has come to develop a new system, one that stimulates job growth, helps the unemployed return to work to become productive contributors to the economy, and still leave intact a financially solvent system that can provide benefits to individuals who have lost their jobs.

I believe it can be done.

Instead of continuing to devise ways to keep paying unemployment benefits for longer periods of time, with compensation that barely meets the basic economic needs of the individual, we need to be focusing our efforts on getting the unemployed back into a legitimate employer–employee relationship. When individuals remain unemployed for extensive periods of time, the resulting impact on people's lives is devastating, and the negative effect on the economy is disastrous. For every week, month, or year that employees remain unemployed, it becomes that much further they fall behind in experience, wage progressions, skill attainment, and benefit accruals. The labor market, as an entity, suffers as well when the collective experience and skill level of the workforce diminishes. Further, when people remain shut out of the traditional employment relationships for long periods of time, they often begin to accept work for wages paid "under the table," or untaxed, while at the same time continuing to receive unemployment benefits. That further depresses the economy deeper into recession. Untaxed wages means the following are not being paid:

- employer-paid Social Security taxes
- employee-paid Social Security taxes
- employer-paid Medicare taxes

- employee-paid Medicare taxes
- federal income taxes
- state and local income taxes (where applicable)
- Workers Compensation premiums
- state unemployment taxes
- federal unemployment taxes

This all points to the fact that long durations of unemployment are not good for *anybody*. They're not good for the economy, they're not good for the government, they're not good for the business community, and they certainly aren't good for the unemployed, most of who just desire someone to give them a decent job.

So let's approach this from a completely different angle. We need to be looking at ways we can create *incentives* for businesses to hire individuals off of unemployment, while at the same time providing those individuals with higher wages than they receive through UI benefits. This can be accomplished *within the current system*. We just need to rethink how we administer the unemployment benefits. It only requires a slight difference in how we pay the unemployed. The difference would be to allow employers to hire individuals off of unemployment and use the unemployment benefits they already receive as part of the total wages paid to the employee. The unemployment benefit payments that are provided to unemployed individuals would continue to be paid even after obtaining a job, but such payments could be used as a wage supplement to the employers that hire them. Additionally, as part of this arrangement, the employer would only be required to match at least 20 percent of the unemployment wages paid to the employee. This insures individuals receive higher wages being employed rather than unemployed. The unemployment benefit payments can continue to be paid directly to the claimant, but the employer would only have to pay the additional 20 percent.

For example, if an employee is receiving $300 in weekly UI benefits, and an employer hires that person, the total weekly wage the employee would receive would be $360 ($300 plus 20 percent). However, the employer would only have to actually pay the additional $60, and the $300 unemployment benefit would continue to be paid to the employee, thus totaling $360 per week. Therefore, the true weekly cost to the employer to employ this individual is only $60 (plus taxes), instead of $360 (plus taxes). This significantly offsets the cost of employing that individual. When employment costs are significantly lowered in this manner, these wage supplements will encourage hiring activity among thousands of employers across the country. When businesses are allowed to hire individuals at drastically reduced labor costs, they will have a very strong incentive to resume hiring. Rather quickly, jobs will begin to appear on the radar screen and the unemployed can begin to flow back into the labor market.

But that is only one aspect of solving this crisis. We still must address how the unemployment funds can begin to be replenished. This can be accomplished as well. Another feature of this system is that we can actually utilize the wage supplement to help restore some financial integrity to the unemployment funds. SUTA and FUTA taxes, as well as FICA, federal, state, and local taxes, would be chargeable to the employer for the full amount of the $360 wage (in the example above). This acts to replenish the unemployment funds, and other government-funded programs, due to the fact that payroll taxes are being paid on the unemployment wages and the subsidy paid to the employee. This is completely unlike the current system, where unemployment benefits are *not* SUTA/FUTA taxed, and thus, no replenishment to the UI funds ever occur. This way, the wage subsidy system allows for taxes to flow back into the system to cover for other benefit obligations. The overall tax burden on businesses will eventually diminish as more and more employees will be employed, there will be less money pulled from the funds overall, and the state funds will begin to recuperate and achieve solvency. Employees who refuse qualified job offers should be disqualified from further UI benefits, and this too will reduce the strain on the funds. If someone is unwilling to return to work, there should be no further unemployment payments to that individual. The unemployment system was never intended to sustain income for long periods of time, and we need to develop a solution that gets individuals off of unemployment as soon as possible. The wage subsidies are intended to do just that.

And the beauty of the whole concept is that the financial resources needed to fund the subsidies are already in place in the form of the current unemployment benefit funds and federal loans, which have already been appropriated by Congress. The money is already allocated to be spent in the form of unemployment benefits, so let's use this money to pay wages to the unemployed *and create jobs at the same time.*

It will be necessary to limit how long employers can claim the wage subsidy, say twenty-six to fifty-two weeks, and there would need to be controls in place that would disallow employers to lay off employees and then rehire them only to get the subsidy, but such controls are not difficult to devise. By capping the subsidy at twenty-six to fifty-two weeks, this also acts to reduce the drain on the UI funds that are now allowing up to two years of UI benefits. Furthermore, re-employment of the unemployed results in actual generation of productive output and value. This is quite contrary to our current system, where we pay individuals to do nothing but look for work. We would create a system where employers could resume hiring at much lower costs, the unemployed could get jobs at higher levels of pay, the unemployment funds would get replenished, local economies would be stimulated, tax bases would be increased for FICA, FUTA, and SUTA, and productive output would be achieved. Employed individuals would purchase and consume more goods and services, and that would spur further business activity, creating more jobs, more sales tax revenues, and so on. There would eventually be fewer and fewer claimants pulling money from the UI funds, and the corresponding reduction in payroll taxes and labor costs for employers would free up more capital for business investment and expansion. All of these factors would feed the cycle of economic recovery, and the impact would be immediate and significant.

Just imagine how this wage subsidy approach to solving the unemployment crisis could have a completely restorative effect on states with double-digit unemployment rates, such as Michigan, Nevada, and many other states so hard hit by the recession. Knowing that the unemployment wages could be used to supplement compensation, start-up companies could flock to those states to create new businesses that could employ thousands of people currently collecting unemployment wages, significantly reducing the start-up costs that are such an impediment to business creation. Knowing that a majority of the wages would be supplemented for a period of time, start-ups might flourish. The push for more investment in "green" jobs could also be stimulated. Existing businesses could also afford to start rehiring some employees who were laid off knowing that their wages would be supplemented by 50 to 80 percent. They are currently unable to rehire those individuals because they can't afford to bring them back at full wage costs. However, even if every business was able to hire just one more person to the payroll, the impact would be dramatic in creating a true economic stimulus. Millions more could be re-employed, millions more could be engaging in more commerce and trade, and millions more could be weaned off the unemployment rolls in a shorter time span, restoring financial integrity to the UI funding mechanisms. The economy would become rapidly converted back into health, and goods and services would begin to flow freely once again. Even General Motors and Chrysler could hire some folks back knowing that a significant portion of the wages would be supplemented for a period of time, allowing them to lower their overall labor costs, produce cars for less money, and increase their profit margins. This just might allow these companies to return some of the taxpayer money that was invested to keep them alive.

However, if we are truly going to solve this crisis and be dedicated to preserving the financial solvency of the system, another systemic reform needs to take place. There must be much tighter controls on who *should* be eligible for unemployment, and we need to move away from our current system of allowing more and more undeserving employees to receive benefits when none should be paid. The new standard for unemployment eligibility needs to be: If you contributed in *any* way to your job loss, your benefits are reduced or eliminated completely. We cannot continue to treat unemployment as a secondary welfare system. It was originally intended as an emergency stopgap financial buffer, for limited duration, offered when employees lost their jobs through layoff or plant closure. But slowly and steadily, we have seen the system evolve into a means by which poor performers, absentee employees, and individuals displaying abhorrent behaviors are allowed to collect unemployment benefits. I can cite hundreds of examples of this that I have witnessed over the years, but let me illustrate my point with just one.

I had just transferred to Alabama with a previous employer, and as the human resources director, I was dealing with an absentee problem with one of our employees. For two years prior to my arrival, and continuing for another year or so after I became involved, this employee had a history of absenteeism and had been issued verbal and written warnings in all of those years regarding her need to improve her attendance. She also had this problem addressed in every single performance review she received during that same time frame. Her pattern was predictable: she would receive her allotted vacation and sick time on January 1 of each year (like all the employees) and she would use up all her paid time during the first half of the year. Then she would continue to miss work, resulting in such time being considered unexcused, which would trigger the various verbal and written warnings. She would be right at the cusp of being terminated but would clean up her act for a short period of time, make it to January 1, get her new allotment of vacation and sick time, and the cycle would repeat itself. Well, the next year she ended up exhausting all of her allotted sick and vacation time in the first three months of the year, leaving her with nine months of calendar time to keep her attendance under control. Needless to say, she did not. We issued the obligatory verbal warnings, written warnings, and finally her last and final written warning stating that *any* further absences would result in immediate termination. She missed work again due to a family crisis, and due to the circumstances and the fact she was emotionally distraught over the incident, we told her to take a week off to recuperate, then return to work, and in lieu of termination, we would issue one last final, final, written warning, and that any further absences would result in her termination. Well, about a month after she returned to work, she called in sick (remember she had exhausted all of her sick and vacation time), and we proceeded to terminate her.

As expected, she filed for unemployment and was awarded eligibility for benefits. I appealed and, for the appeals hearing, went armed with all of the documents proving she had been verbally warned, written up, counseled during her reviews, etc. As I was full into my Perry Mason-like presentation of the facts, I was interrupted by the hearing officer, who asked, "Mr. Sinas, does your company have a policy regarding calling in sick?" "Yes, we do," I replied. "And did she follow those procedures?" "Yes, she did." "Did you have any reason to believe she was not sick?" "No, it really didn't matter if she was sick or not. She was absent yet again, and as our final warning indicated, regardless of the reason, *any* further absence would result in immediate termination," I explained. "Yes, but are you aware that in the state of Alabama, if the last absence that led to termination was due to illness, the claimant is automatically eligible for unemployment?"

I sat there, not sure if I was more surprised and bewildered or just plain ticked off, and I asked, "Are you telling me that the four years, *four years,* of absenteeism, and four years of disciplining this employee for this serious problem, are irrelevant? You mean to tell me that in spite of all of those warnings, and in spite of all the times she failed to show up for work for reasons *not associated with illness,* and in spite of all the times she caused production delays due to those absences, none of that is considered when determining eligibility for unemployment benefits? And now, after we have been trying for over four years to get her to come to work to earn a living, the state of Alabama will now allow her to sit at home and do nothing and be paid for it. Is that what you are telling me?" "Yes, sir," she stated, *"that's the law."*

And so it is.

Our unemployment system has been transformed into a safety net for the employees who have been terminated for cause, who have displayed a total lack of concern for their employer, and who are undeserving of payments to be *unemployed* when they already had a job that would have continued to employ and pay them had they only done two simple things—show up for work and perform their job duties as required. When those standards are not met, employers should not be forced by our government to pay that individual *not* to work. We should never reward absenteeism and poor performance with unemployment benefits.

The continuing practice of paying unemployment benefits to poor performers and absentee employees has led to the accelerated depletion of the funds available to truly deserving employees, and it must stop. We have created a system that rewards lack of effort and misconduct, and acts to encourage lengthy stays on unemployment rolls. This can be significantly curtailed by disallowing benefit payments to those who contributed to their job loss and limiting the total duration of UI payments to deserving and eligible employees for twenty-six weeks. Extensions could be considered in certain circumstances but must be limited to job losses associated with mass layoffs, business closures and recessionary economic conditions. Even in those conditions, unemployment benefits should not be extended beyond 52 weeks. The system simply cannot sustain employees who have been terminated for cause, and it should instead be available to those who have lost jobs through reasons that are not within the control of the affected employees. This in itself will be a significant aspect of solving the unemployment underfunding crisis. But Congress wants to do just the opposite and allow currently employed individuals to be able to voluntarily quit their jobs because of personal reasons and receive unemployment benefits from an already strained system. In their minds, it's perfectly acceptable because the business community will ultimately pay for it.

The subsidy solution is the proverbial win-win scenario and helps reduce taxes and solve the underfunding that will soon result in a total systemic collapse if we continue to keep the status quo. If our state and federal government *truly* want to create a stimulus for jobs *and* reduce tax burdens *and* solve the unemployment crisis, this system is a blueprint to lead the way. Even unions will benefit, as they will see their members rehired in greater numbers, resulting in higher dues collection into their coffers. In reality, it is the *business community* that pays for the unemployment system in almost every state in the union, so it should rightfully be returned to them so they can use that money they once possessed to create jobs. I can't think of a better way than to allow businesses to recoup some of those costs, while at the same time provide our citizens with further employment opportunities, pay them more than they would receive on unemployment, and stimulate economic expansion. *Everyone wins.*

President Obama said in one of his first weekly address to the nation on January 24, 2009, that "experts agree that if nothing is done, the unemployment rate could reach double digits ..." The only way to prevent unemployment from reaching double digits, Obama said, was to pass the stimulus bill that would cost over 780 billion dollars. He claimed the stimulus would keep unemployment rates below 8 percent. We have seen the results. The stimulus passed, unemployment exceeded 10 percent, and our politicians are more focused on passing massive health care reform that will cost another trillion dollars rather than working on ways to help businesses recover so that they may begin to re-employ our workers.

More recently, President Obama held a "jobs summit" in an effort to devise ways to put America back to work. The result was, in my opinion, a dismal failure. The resulting "solutions" were unoriginal and uninspired. Washington's answer to creating jobs involved more stimulus money for infrastructure improvements (e.g. roads, bridges, etc.); tax breaks for small businesses, and tax incentives to encourage people to make their homes more energy efficient. That was it. That was the solution to creating jobs. First of all, very few jobs will be created by providing tax rebates to people who improve the energy efficiency of their homes. It appears that Washington is proposing that when we provide taxpayer-funded rebates to people to spend money on items they probably can't afford, (i.e. more energy efficient air conditioners, windows, etc.), we will see millions of Americans put back to work. Sign me up as totally unconvinced this will have any significant impact on reducing unemployment.

Secondly, the idea that infrastructure improvements will create jobs may have some positive effect in creating certain jobs, but those jobs will be confined to the construction sector, not the overall business spectrum. Further, as we have already witnessed with the first stimulus package, the funding necessary to get "shovel ready" projects off the ground has been slow in materializing and often mired in bureaucratic red tape before it actually gets disbursed. This method of job creation has proven to be inefficient and confined to only a limited portion of the economy. Just recently, and article by Matt Apuzzo and Brett J. Blackledge, distributed by the Associated Press (January 12, 2010) indicated that "an Associated Press analysis of stimulus spending found that it didn't matter if a lot of money was spent on highways or none at all: Local unemployment rates rose and fell regardless. And the stimulus only barely helped the beleaguered construction industry, the analysis showed…AP's analysis, which was reviewed by independent economists at five universities showed the strategy of pumping transportation money into counties hasn't affected local unemployment rates so far. "

If we want to create jobs across all business sectors, the wage subsidy proposal presented herein does just that. It allows *all* businesses to benefit, because all businesses will have access to the subsidy. It will not be confined to the construction industry, the "green jobs" industry, or the banking industry. It is an equal opportunity employer, and it will benefit significantly more businesses and unemployed individuals. It is an approach that can truly have the effect of kick starting the economy because it is all inclusive. We do not need to stimulate only fragments of the economy, but the economy in its entirety. Tax breaks help, but do nothing to give employers needed money to fund jobs *immediately*.

I ask that Washington give due consideration to this approach to solving the unemployment crisis. We are already allocating funds to the unemployed, and most of those people want to get back to work. Businesses want to hire folks back, but they need some help with labor costs. The current system does nothing to stimulate jobs; as a matter of fact, it stimulates further unemployment. There are over fifteen million people currently unemployed in the United States (source: Bureau of Labor Statistics, December 2009). Our national unemployment rate in November 2009 was 10.2 percent according to federal records, not counting those who have given up hope and stopped looking for work, or those who are underemployed. If we could create meaningful jobs for just 30 percent of the unemployed, we could put five million more people back to work. A 50-percent increase in jobs could put over seven million Americans back to work. The economy could steadily come back to life, employing more and more of the unemployed. Much can be gained, and nothing can be lost. If this system is implemented, the worst thing that could happen is that millions of Americans will be put back to work for a limited period of time, but then placed back on unemployment because the economy failed to recover sufficiently. However, while the system was in place, businesses were able to utilize labor at significantly reduced cost, individuals that were hired enjoyed higher wages for a period of time, tax collections increased, and our unemployment funds received additional revenue. And this would have all been accomplished with no additional taxes or additional congressional funding. So, at its very worst outcome, we are still better off than where we find ourselves currently.

However, if it works, which I am convinced it can, we will revive our economy, put millions back to work, and allow for many of the unemployed to be permanently absorbed back into the labor market as businesses and the economy begin to recover. It is not intended to be a permanent arrangement, but rather a comprehensive kick start to the economy where all business sectors can benefit at the same time, hopefully resulting in long term recovery and sustainable employment levels. This is a change that makes sense. Let's get business and government working together to implement this system that is truly focused on getting our nation back to work. And while we're at it, let's talk to the unemployed and see if they will be willing to back a proposal that is designed to get them re-employed. My guess is that they are ready for a new solution, one that is focused on creating jobs and returning them to work, not further entrenching them in jobless hell where current government policies keep them.

OTHER RECOMMENDED REFORMS

I am a firm believer in the fact that reform in the workplace is a two-way street. The business community is also in significant need of changing their ways in how they manage their companies and, more specifically, how they manage their employees. I addressed earlier the importance of human capital management and how critical it is to recruit, employ, and retain the very best employees and, just as importantly, the need to shed employees who are not adding any significant value to the enterprise. But as critical as those factors are in determining the relative success or failure of any given business, most organizations do a terrible job at developing and implementing human capital management strategies. So reform is also necessary in the business community. They need to improve significantly in their ability to recruit top talent and become much more adept at managing that talent to insure the highest levels of performance are consistently achieved. Business leaders must learn how to better link high levels of performance to competitive and effective compensation practices, and they must develop systems that allow for the identification and ejection of unsatisfactory performers. So to be fair, I feel that the next major piece of reform (following closely behind the unemployment reforms mentioned above) is to require businesses to adopt a changing set of practices relating to the management of their employees. In a bold move to offer the olive branch to Congress as a sign that we are serious about changing the face of how this country conducts business, I propose we eliminate the concept of "at-will employment."

The doctrine of at-will employment basically stipulates that:

> an employee may enter into an employment relationship with any given employer, at any time, and for any reason; and that same employee may terminate the employment reason at any time, for any reason, or no reason at all. Conversely, employers may also enter into an employment relationship with a willing employee, at any time, and for any reason; and that same employer may also terminate the employment relationship at any time, for any lawful reason, or no reason at all, with or without cause or prior notice.

This obviously gives employers the right to terminate their employees at any time, with or without cause, and even for no reason whatsoever. The right to "employ at will" is legally protected in over two-thirds of the states in the United States.

There are undoubtedly many reading this right now from the business community who must think I've lost my marbles to offer up the holy grail of employee management, and they probably wish at this moment to pluck my eyeballs out with a sharp object. After all, I am proposing to eliminate the only morsel of legal protection that is afforded to business relating to employment. But as they say, there is a method to my madness. I propose we eliminate "employment at will" *if* the other reforms mentioned earlier and subsequently are adopted by Congress and embraced by the courts. So let's map this out as to how we can all get on board—Congress, the Courts, and the business community—so that we can improve the health of the economy and the personal success of those who deserve it most.

At-Will Employment

I've heard too many captains of business exclaim how they can hire and fire anybody they want, and if they choose to terminate someone, they don't *have* to give a reason. Legally, that's true to some degree. However, you can still be sued for terminating someone, and if you choose to offer up to a jury that the reason you fired someone was for "no reason at all," good luck convincing twelve peers of that poor mistreated employee that the employer was justified in his actions. Juries decide cases on emotion, and you have two strikes against you if you wish to stipulate that you legally don't have to provide a reason for the termination. But the main reason I think businesses should never rely on at-will employment as a means to make employment decisions is that I believe it's cowardly. I don't believe there should *ever* be a termination decision that doesn't have a justifiable reason behind it. If the employment relationship must end due to the economic condition of the business, then explain that to the employee. If the termination decision is due to performance deficiencies, those deficiencies should be discussed and documented while they occur, and the employee should be told exactly what repercussions will follow if performance expectations are not met. If the termination is due to violation of policy, the policy first should have been disseminated to employees before they can be held accountable for adhering to it. There certainly may be behaviors exhibited by employees that are so severe or inappropriate that it warrants immediate termination, but those reasons should still be stipulated at termination.

The point is, effective management means communicating to employees *what* needs to be done, training them on *how* it should be done, indicating *when* it needs to be accomplished, and explaining *why* it's important to perform the job responsibilities properly. Furthermore, the employee needs to understand what will occur if performance expectations are not met. Effective management means developing performance measurement systems to allow for the documentation of both poor and exceptional performance, communicating to all employees their strengths and weaknesses, and offering guidance on how to improve on both. It means developing employees into highly effective contributors and eliminating those who fail to contribute in any significant manner. Effective management means knowing how to develop recruiting systems that accurately identify individuals who possess the appropriate skills, abilities, attitudes, and track records necessary to be high-value employees. So, if the business community wants to really get it right, toss aside the reliance on at-will employment and instead rely on effective human capital management practices. But for the business community to loosen their grip on at-will employment legal protections, they must be given a permanent reprieve from the burdensome costs associated with frivolous allegations of wrongdoing. Therefore, my recommendation is to prohibit employers from utilizing at-will employment as a means to justify employment actions, but also incorporate a system that allows for employers to be shielded from meritless allegations and lawsuits, if they can prove just cause for their decisions.

To provide the necessary protections from frivolous charges and to level the playing field just a bit, the charging party must have a financial stake in the outcome. The employer should be held responsible for paying compensatory damages if the allegations are proven to be merited and even punitive damages if the employer's actions are found to be egregious. Conversely, employees making allegation of improprieties must also be held responsible for the employer's costs associated with the defense of the allegations, if such allegations are found to be meritless or frivolous. That provides some balance to the system. Hold the employer accountable for justifying the employment decisions made, but also hold the employee accountable for paying the costs incurred by the employer if indeed the employer can show that the employment actions were reasonable and justifiable. This can be accomplished with the following reforms.

Title VII

It is time to rescind Title VII—not because I am against anti-discrimination laws, but because I believe it is time we move beyond looking at race, age, gender, and all of the other so-called "protected classes." I believe *all* employees should be protected from arbitrary and indefensible employment decisions and actions. I can't help but recall the words of Dr. Martin Luther King when he was pleading for America to abandon their prejudicial ways and to reach a point where people "can be judged not by the color of their skin, but by the content of their character." Dr. King spoke of a universal ideal that challenged us to value the merits of the individual, regardless of race or color, irrespective of gender or age, and blind to the disabilities one might have. If we wish to *truly* move this society to a color-blind status, then we must quit considering race, color, gender, and all of the other subcategories of the human race and start only considering the condition of someone's character as the measuring tool. And the employment arena is exactly the place to begin this transformation. It is time we stopped categorizing our workforce as "black employees" or "white employees" or "female employees" or "older employees" and start categorizing employees by their skills, abilities, knowledge, education, past experience, demonstrated performance, exhibited behaviors, value contributions, and adherence to expectations. It moves us away from the categorization that Title VII forces upon the workplace—namely, the emphasis on *what* someone is rather than how they perform. We need an employment law system that forces employers to justify their employment actions based upon the criteria of skills, abilities, performance, and behaviors versus race, age, sex, color, etc. The *new* law that should govern the workplace would stipulate:

> Employers may terminate employment, demote from a position, refuse to promote, or refuse to hire an employee *only when*:
> - an applicant for employment has demonstrated a lack of skills, abilities, knowledge, experience, acceptable past performance, and/or required education to perform the job as stipulated by the employer, or has demonstrated such to a lesser degree than other applicants, including responses to interview inquiries and questions posed to all applicants.
> - an employee has demonstrated performance deficiencies or failed to properly perform the required tasks as defined in the job description.
> - an employee has violated documented policies, rules of conduct, or expected levels of behavior, or has acted in disregard for the safety of employees, the employer's property, and/or the well-being of the company.
> - employees do not possess the necessary skills, abilities, knowledge, experience, acceptable performance, and/or education to be considered for advancement, or have demonstrated such to a lesser degree than other candidates, including responses to interview inquiries and questions posed to all candidates.
> - the economic conditions of the company or financial performance requires headcount adjustments, layoffs, job elimination, job restructuring, and/or reassignment to other positions, and such decisions are made by demonstrated and documented performance, skills,

> abilities, and/or educational differences between otherwise qualified employees, and when all things are deemed equal, seniority shall prevail.

Employers who fail to properly document and/or demonstrate through objective data deficiencies in performance, skills, abilities, education, or economic reversals can be subject to charges, fines, penalties, punitive damages, and/or compensatory damages to the affected employee/applicant if no justification for the employment action can be produced.

That's it. That's the replacement for anti-discrimination laws. It requires employers to properly manage their workplaces by communicating rules of conduct, expected levels of behavior, workplace policies, performance expectations, and repercussions for unacceptable performance. I would retain the current regulations regarding the prohibition against workplace harassment and require businesses to have policies and systems in place where employees may voice complaints of unwelcome conduct by management, co-workers, customers, and vendors. Such conduct would include sexual harassment, racial harassment, and other related behaviors that are abusive and/or intimidating toward employees. Additionally, I believe we should continue to require reasonable accommodation for disabled employees/applicants but refine the law so that employers may directly communicate with the physician treating the disability so that better efforts can be made to formulate proper accommodations. The main focus regarding disabilities, however, must remain on the ability to perform the essential functions of the job, with or without reasonable accommodation, and stop attempting to categorize every ailment, condition, impairment and abnormality to such a degree that it creates barriers for businesses to expect acceptable attendance and performance levels.

Many will argue that I am attempting to turn back the clock on strides we've made on discrimination. However, I contend I'm doing just the opposite. I want this country to move beyond looking at individuals as white, black, old, young, Muslim, Christian, etc. I want employers to focus on the contributions individuals make regardless of those characteristics. We need to remove the system of segmenting everyone into these pigeonholes if we are really interested in treating all individuals based only upon their contributions and character. In this new world of employment law, any employer who continues to make discriminatory employment decisions would be subjected to potential liability if they failed to prove that their decisions were related to performance, skills, abilities, etc. If an employer says, "You're fired because you are black," or, "You're fired because you are gay," those decisions would be still be illegal, and the employer would be liable. There would be no need to prove racial animosity or bias toward sexual preference because that would be irrelevant. If the employer could not show the employment action was rooted in documented differences in performance, skill, ability, qualification for the job, irresponsible behavior, or economic conditions of the company, then the action could be legally challenged.

Even when layoffs occur, the employer would be required to demonstrate why any certain individual was terminated while others were not. The burden on the employer would be to prove that layoff decisions were based upon an analysis of relative skill, ability, performance, etc., regarding all of the employees affected. The race, color, age, gender, sexual preference, or national origin of the employee won't matter because that would not be the criteria on which illegal employment actions would be judged. We need to stop trying to get inside the business owner's head to see if he harbors some sort of prejudice against one group of individuals or another and focus solely on the business justification of his employment decisions. If the business owner cannot put forth a compelling argument as to why Billy and Susie were fired, demoted, or not hired, then he's got a legal problem, regardless of his so-called hidden motives. This is truly color-blind justice in the workplace.

These changes obviously would necessitate proper documentation methods, performance measurement systems, and communication of expectations. In other words, it would be exactly what is missing in most businesses today, and that's sound human resource management practices. By improving how we manage our employees, we take huge leaps in not only improving our bottom line, but also in our ability to compete, grow, hire, and competitively compensate more employees. Through effective management practices, we also build a wall of protection around us that repels the slings and arrows of meritless allegations launched at us by disgruntled employees who refuse to accept the fact that they were terminated because of their own failings, not management's. If the new law requires proof of justifiable actions, truly effective managers would consider that to be an easy standard to meet and would have no problems producing the necessary justification. It would now be incumbent upon the employee to examine if indeed there was an unjust employment practice, and further, determine whether they feel they could prevail in an employment action against the employer. If they are willing to accept some of the risk if they lose, but are convinced nonetheless that they have a case, charges could be filed, but under a newly remodeled system described below.

The Equal Employment Opportunity Commission (EEOC)
The EEOC is the governmental regulatory agency that processes and investigates employment discrimination claims that are filed under Title VII. This agency also has the authority to initiate litigation on behalf of the charging party against any company that allegedly engages in the prohibited conduct under the law. However, as with any government agency, it is a bureaucratic monstrosity that is inefficient and wasteful. The incident I described earlier regarding my first unemployment claim I handled in Alabama has a "Part 2" component to that story:

Soon after I lost my unemployment hearing regarding her claim, I received a letter in the mail from the EEOC (which tends to always make your day). The EEOC was undertaking an investigation of a race discrimination charge from that same woman—you remember, the one with four years of absenteeism. She was alleging that she was actually terminated because of her race and that there was another employee of a different race who had absenteeism problems, but he was *not* fired. EEOC then demanded the submission of documents, personnel files, and statistics showing all terminations due to absenteeism, broken down by the race of each terminated employee. In addition, we had to provide a position statement responding to each of her allegations.

Now, what makes this story even more interesting is that the woman we fired for absenteeism is white. Her discrimination charge stated that we had an employee who was black who also had absence problems, but he was not terminated; therefore, our decision was based upon race, not for the reasons we indicated. First of all, there indeed was a black employee who did have an absenteeism problem, but his situation was different in the fact that he did not have as many absences as she did, he did not have a past history of absences like she did, and he was only at the written warning stage of the disciplinary process. But more to the point, her allegation that our decision to terminate her because she was white was so outlandish that I really thought it was a joke and just a way for her to force us to have to spend time and money to answer the charges. I honestly believed that once I submitted the information to the EEOC, they would see through her scam and drop the charges. I was dead wrong.

Upon submission of our position statement (her personnel file, the personnel files of other terminated employees, and all of the written documentation we had regarding her absences), we heard nothing from the EEOC for over six months. Finally, I received another letter from them requesting further data and information. I was flabbergasted. How in the world was the EEOC blind to the fact that we had more than ample justification for her termination? I continued to play the game, providing the additional information and waiting again for their findings. After an additional nine months, I received notification that, due to the case backlog at the EEOC, case disposition was behind schedule and there would be further delays in reaching a final determination regarding this charge.

Okay, let's just stop here for a moment and review the situation. We have a terminated employee who had over four years of absenteeism, a personnel file full of documented warnings and performance reviews admonishing her to improve her attendance or face termination, and statistics that showed our terminations for absenteeism were not biased toward one race or another. That in and of itself should have ended the investigation. Now throw in the fact that she is claiming race discrimination because she is white. All of the individuals involved in the termination decision were also white. Yet the EEOC still is carrying on with investigating this completely bogus charge. I have literally never had more evidence and documentation on any single employee that I have ever terminated than her. But the EEOC was reluctant to believe we acted justifiably, seemingly insisting that our true motives were to fire this employee because … she was white. I can assure you there was no meeting of the minds of our management staff where we all said, "It has come to the point where we need to get rid of Lucy because … you know … she's white, and we just can't have white folks working here." Anyway, after handling this case for over sixteen months, the EEOC finally issued their determination, stating that they could find no cause in supporting her allegations of discrimination. I thought to myself, "no kidding. It took sixteen months to arrive at that conclusion?" The fact that they had binders full of substantiated evidence of a justifiable termination was still insufficient to conclude this case should have been thrown out from the moment they received our first submission. Apparently, it was deemed appropriate to waste our time, resources, and money, as well as taxpayer dollars, pursuing a frivolous charge.

But wait, there's more …

After the EEOC issued its findings, they also issued to the claimant, as required by law, the infamous "right to sue" letter. This letter stipulates that an employee has ninety days to file additional charges against the employer in a court of law (the double jeopardy situation I alluded to earlier) if she so chooses. To make matters worse, some federal courts have recently ruled that the EEOC retains the right to remain involved in the case even after the charging party has received the right-to-sue letter and has initiated a lawsuit. Well, on day eighty-eight of this time frame, I received yet another letter, this time from an attorney, claiming he was representing her in a case against our company and alleging that we discriminated against her because of her race and due to her disability. Disability? What disability? This woman was no more disabled than I was, and yet she is adding this claim to her already-frivolous charge of race discrimination. So here we go again. I had to retain defense counsel to answer the charges, we were forced to submit more documents, personnel files, and statistics, and answer interrogatories for the attorney so he could attempt to build a case against us. Our defense counsel petitioned the courts for summary judgment (basically a bench decision from the courts without the trial), and after about six more months, the court issued a summary judgment in our favor and the case was tossed. Practically *two years* justifying our termination decision to regulatory agencies, government personnel, attorneys, and judges, all for them to arrive at the same very startling conclusion—she deserved to be fired for absenteeism.

This is the system our government has created. This is the inefficient and cumbersome process that punishes even the innocent businesses that are only trying to make employment decisions that are in the best interest of the company and its employees. This is the type of governmental bullying directed at businesses that is conducted on a regular basis, all in the name of …employee justice.

I am a firm believer in the fact that wronged employees need to have a forum to voice their grievances, attempt resolution, and be compensated if there was a significant lack of justification for the employment action. However, employers should also have access to a legal system that allows them to defend charges of discrimination, and if there is ample evidence showing the employment decision was justifiable, the charging party, or the plaintiff's attorney who pursued a frivolous charge, should be legally required to pay the out-of-pocket expenses the employer incurs as part of the defense of these claims. Employers should not be forced to justify every employment decision that gets challenged by current or ex-employees without having the opportunity to recoup the cost associated with these challenges if they are determined to be unfounded. This can be accomplished with a modification of the current process, and the EEOC can be made more effective and efficient with some changes to its stated purpose and system of investigation. The agency should only be involved in four things:

1. Processing complaints from employees who allege they unjustifiably suffered an adverse employment action.
2. Investigating the alleged complaints to determine if the employer was justified in his decision, whether the employee contributed in any way to the adverse action, and whether there were any indications of intent on the employer's part to act without concern for fairness or reasonableness.
3. Mediating between the parties to attempt resolution that would be acceptable to both.
4. Developing a written analysis of the allegations and stipulating the relative strengths of the positions put forth by both the charging party and the employer (if unable to reach a mutually agreeable settlement of the allegations). This written analysis shall conclude with a relative "score" regarding the merits of the

allegations and the reasonableness of the employers' actions. A score of fifty would mean that there was equal culpability on the part of both the employee and the employer. A score of one hundred would indicate the allegations put forth by the employee could be proven with objective evidence that showed the employer acted egregiously and without concern for fairness or reasonableness. A score of zero would indicate that the allegations were *totally without merit* and were fabricated to cover for the fact that the employer had ample justification for his actions and the decision was well reasoned and justifiable on all accounts.

Once the EEOC issues its findings, employees may elect to pursue the charges in court. However, if the allegations scored at a fifty or lower, and the employee still wishes to pursue the charges in court, then if the employee eventually loses his challenge in court, he would be responsible for the costs incurred by the employer in defending the charges. Conversely, if the EEOC scores the case at higher than fifty, and the employer is still reluctant to settle at mediation, then if the employer loses the case, he would be subject to penalties and damages awarded to the employee by the court, plus punitive damages if the case was scored at seventy or higher by the EEOC. This keeps frivolous charges out of court, allows employers some measure of protection against exploitive settlement demands, and creates a balanced system that encourages settlement when both parties share in the blame for the adverse employment action. This will also help drastically reduce the consistent backlog of cases for the EEOC. As of September 30, 2009, the EEOC case backlog was 85,768 charges, a 15-percent increase over the previous year. The system is slow and inefficient and contributes to delayed justice for both the employee and the employer. But government wants to expand the EEOC bureaucracy and add an additional 125 investigators, 22 trial attorneys, and 50 additional staff members. These hires would not be necessary, and the cost to the taxpayer would be nullified if we structure the EEOC as proposed.

Nowhere in this model does the EEOC retain policy-making authority or prosecutorial powers. The agency would exist to protect both employers and employees. If, as the current system allows, employees can file a charge with the EEOC, and subsequently file it in court anyway, then we might as well remove the redundancy of the system and just have the courts make the final decision as to the merits of the case. The EEOC then acts as an intermediary, a government entity that works to eliminate unjust workplace decisions, but also acts to protect businesses from baseless claims. Their investigations should be impartial and designed to determine what really transpired in the situation at hand. Their recommendations would carry much weight with the court but could be overruled if the court deemed their arguments unpersuasive or inaccurate. The courts should also have the authority to require the EEOC to pay for the costs incurred by either party if it is determined that their handling of the case was so poor that it might be considered negligent or irresponsible. Within that type of system, all parties involved have a stake in the outcome. But the new standard by which all is measured is: did the employer have justifiable and reasonable cause to take the employment action that occurred? If the answer is yes, the employer needs to be shielded from liability, and the employee needs to be prevented from engaging in litigation lottery where he seeks one forum after another in order to extract undeserved compensation from the employer.

But our current system does nothing of the sort. When employees file totally baseless claims, they are still allowed free access to our government institutions, funded by taxpayer money. And when all the dust settles and the facts of the case show the employer did not engage in prohibited conduct whatsoever, the employee making the trumped-up allegations is the only one who doesn't lose anything. If the ultimate goal is to allow employees their day in court, then appoint the EEOC as the fact finders for the court and the agency responsible for weeding out claims that can be settled without judicial intervention. But strip them of their authority to prosecute on their own, for they only wield that power against employers and never employees.

The current system was established as a mechanism to allow employees to file complaints against employers for alleged acts of discrimination or unlawful behavior. Our government agencies then fervently pursue charges and attempt to impose repercussions on the employer if they believe questionable conduct occurred. But there is an absence of concern for the business that has been wronged by an employee. Congress has shown an apparent disregard for the fact that poor performance or negligence by employees can have very damaging effects on business operations. Excessive errors, scrap, absenteeism, theft, embezzlement, destruction of property, violent behavior, drug abuse, intoxication, excessive conflicts, insubordination, work disruption, unsafe work habits, and dishonesty are just some of the issues employers must deal with regarding their employees, and all can result in loss of customers, loss of revenue, diminished profits, harm to co-workers, and other devastating consequences. But the employer has no government-created forum to allow the business to recoup such losses. Employees cannot be sued by employers, they can only be fired (or prosecuted), but when employers take those steps, they often find themselves still having to defend charges of discrimination or wrongful termination. The current system is not about workplace justice, it's about arming employees with weapons that can be used against their employer. If the employee has nothing to lose, there is no incentive to refrain from making allegations against the business. We could dispose of many more of the EEOC's backlogged cases if employees knew that they had a financial obligation to pay for costs if they lost a case against an employer who acted reasonably. It will also reduce the caseload of the courts. Our current system of having two avenues of litigation just doubles the efforts, doubles the time, doubles the cost, and doubles the abuse of the system.

It reminds me of a T-shirt I once saw a friend wear that said, "Department of Redundancy Department"—it is a fitting description of our employment law system.

CONCLUSION AND CALL TO ACTION

I do not advocate the elimination of employment laws, I do not recommend we outlaw unions, and I do not wish to see employers operate without reasonable constraints. Employer abuses were the catalyst that brought about calls for government intervention in the workplace and, left unchecked, abusive employment practices may very well return to some degree. Many of the laws that govern the workplace are both needed and justifiable. But the pendulum has swung far to the other side, long bypassing the need to restrain abuses, and moving well into the area of mandating that employees' wants and desires be met. Congress further wants employers to provide ongoing compensation for employees who have personal misfortunes that require them to quit their jobs. This is not the government's role.

Free-market competition should dictate what employers must do to attract and retain the best talent. To remain competitive, employers will have to develop competitive compensation and benefit package as well as vacation and time-off policies that will facilitate the recruitment and retention of star performers. It will be incumbent upon management to develop effective strategies that keep employees motivated, productive, and efficient. Employers must master the art of employee recruitment and development, and they must create work environments that foster creativity, teamwork, growth, and enjoyment. They must also develop a low tolerance for mediocrity, as that is the number-one killer of competitiveness and longevity. Businesses must behave responsibly toward their employees, treating them respectfully, professionally, and fairly. Their employment decisions should not be arbitrary and pointless, but instead be well reasoned and justifiable. Business owners need to bear a responsibility to their employees to always act in the best interest of the business and in the best interest of those who contribute to its success.

But employees carry a large load themselves. They must put forth their best efforts and refrain from engaging in behaviors that lead to waste, errors, scrap, higher costs, and lower profits. They must perform the work as assigned by the employer, and do so in ways that create value and substantive contribution. They must show up for work as scheduled and, when at work, perform their job with pride, dedication, and always with the thought in mind that the quality of the result will be directly proportional to the quality of the effort put forth. If they fail to do so, their jobs should in no way be protected and the employee should not be able to extract financial settlements from the employer who made a reasonable employment decision.

And our government—Congress, the courts, and the White House—must remove the barriers and roadblocks that alter this balance. Moreover, they need to enact legislation that *prevents* this system from getting out of balance because, if it does, the economy and the country suffer greatly. Businesses become less competitive, profits evaporate, jobs are eliminated, and our citizens and families suffer for it. But it is evident that just the opposite is taking place. Government wants more and more control over the workplace, causing irreparable harm in the process. They promote counterproductive policy that rewards lack of effort, poor performance, and incompetence. They wish to punish the successful in order to reward the lazy and unproductive. They stifle efficiency and encourage waste. They create policy that creates further unemployment, not job stimulus. The time is getting late, and our country is on the brink of falling further into the inescapable hole where innovation, entrepreneurship, creativity, and hard work will soon be buried.

The debate about health care reform is another shining example of the desire of government to increase their control over businesses. To give an indication of how our politicians view the role of business in health care reform, proposals from both the House and the Senate require businesses to pay significant taxes to help pay for these reforms, or they mandate that the employer carry health insurance for its employees. We need reforms in the health care system. But needing reforms is a far cry from having the government take control over significant parts of the health care delivery system and then dictating what businesses and individuals must purchase. We know this is a very complex issue with many integrated parts that contribute to the problem. Insurers, providers, patients, lawyers, pharmaceutical companies, hospitals, government agencies, taxpayers, and the uninsured all play a role in this crisis. The system has evolved into a complex web of competing interests and allied forces. The problem cannot be solved easily or quickly, and it will require a tremendous amount of input and analysis from many facets of our society.

Yet, Congress nevertheless crafted a bill that is over two thousand pages that is designed to "fix" this problem. The president himself has indicated time and time again how important this issue is and how complex the task at hand really is. He says he is truly interested in solving this issue, which he says is the main hurdle to ever balancing our budget. On one hand he claims how important it is to get right, but on the other hand, we witness his support of legislation being hastily crafted, without bi-partisan support, and rushed through both houses of congress, even when most Americans are skeptical at best regarding the reforms that are being advocated. We cannot possibly take such a complex issue, hand it over to government bureaucrats, and think we are actually going to see true reforms take root to solve this crisis. It is yet another move to impose more and more control over our businesses and our citizens.

This is more evidence of how government continues to reach into areas they do not understand, yet nonetheless attempt to establish themselves as regulators. This is not only ineffective, but it costs our nation billions of dollars whenever the government establishes a presence. President Obama claimed health care expansions will all be paid for with new premiums on the uninsured and through the reforms that will be made to Medicare and Medicaid, by eliminating waste, fraud, and abuse. Here's an idea. Before we turn over our whole health care system to government control, let's require proof that government can actually affect those reforms to Medicare and Medicaid, and then analyze the results as to how effective they really were in saving money and streamlining those agencies into more efficient entities.

Let's solve this issue one step at a time so that we don't make costly and irreversible mistakes that will have to be paid for by the taxpayers. If health care reform is passed, consider the massive amount of government regulations that will still have to be enacted just to delineate how each governmental agency will act, the authority they posses, and the methods of how services are to be delivered. That legislation has not even seen the light of day, and no one knows how this system will be crafted from top to bottom. But these are the details that none of us have seen, even though they will be the road maps to how this system will operate. This will create new agencies, departments, commissions, systems, rules, laws, enforcement activity, and on and on and on it goes. There is a strong stench of a "trust me" component to the unknown details of this massive undertaking, but Congress has rarely given us any reason whatsoever to give them our trust. And we are told that this will be done with utmost efficiency and will not add a dime to our deficit. I don't believe that.

I was watching the "O'Reilly Factor" the other day when I heard him ask someone, "Are you afraid of your government?" That is an interesting question. After a bit of reflection, I realized my answer would be, "You're damn right I am." I fear further governmental intrusion in our lives, when history has proven time and time again that governmental involvement in *any* endeavor is *never* efficient, *always* more costly, and perpetually frustrating to deal with. Consider that Medicare, Medicaid, and Social Security are all government-run programs and all are nearing insolvency. The government has a terrible track record of allowing entitlement programs and government bureaucracies to become bloated, inefficient, financially mismanaged, and a constant drain on the taxpayer. I would like just one single example of a circumstance where the government managed any element of our economy more effectively than the private sector ever did. Name one. But, for the sake of political expediency, our governmental leaders are biting at the bit to enact legislation that will impact the lives of every American and have significant implications for decades to come. We need to question why our government would act so hastily when it's so obvious that we need more time to properly consider the various options to solving the health care crisis. We need to question why the government continues to insist on further encroachment into our marketplace, our businesses, and our jobs when such interference is proven to be ineffective, counterproductive, and damaging to all parties—except politicians.

We must act now. Business, labor, employees, and concerned citizens need to stop this trend of omnipresent government that, left unchecked, will continue to assume more and more control of the free market and lead to economic chaos. We can begin by implementing the reforms mentioned herein. Shore up the unemployment system as recommended and create incentives for job creation that will put millions back to work now. Inject a level of fairness to the system of litigation related to workplace claims and create barriers to frivolous charges and lawsuits. Remove "protected classes" from employment laws, and start protecting *everyone* from any adverse employment action that is based on anything but requisite skills, abilities, demonstrated performance, prohibited behaviors, and/or economic conditions of the business. Remove mandates on employers that are unconstitutional and indefensible. But most importantly, stop treating businesses as if they are the enemy! Stop immediately this continual onslaught of complex and difficult to understand regulations that burden businesses with costly compliance efforts and operational difficulties. Allow the business owner and the free market to determine relative compensation levels, benefit offerings, time off policies and the like, and permit those decisions to be based upon the businesses ability to pay for them. Above all, give businesses more latitude to make employment decisions without the constant threat of having to defend every aspect of those decisions to government bureaucrats.

Our businesses are the backbone of our economy. They create jobs, provide compensation and benefits, support charities, and sustain our communities. Businesses fund and support research and development projects that result in the invention of new technologies and the discovery of medical breakthroughs. Businesses sustain a stable tax base so that we can provide services to our citizens, protect our property, and provide security to our nation. It's high time the business community and the workforce lets their voice be heard and stand together to elect politicians who are dedicated to helping build business and jobs, and shine light on the politicians who promote further dissemination of taxpayer-funded government handouts to the undeserving. If government continues to enact laws that act to stifle and punish business, then politicians will be to blame for the increased throngs of Americans out of work. They will be responsible for the continued decline in our ability to compete in the global marketplace and their actions will adversely impact our ability to provide a standard of living that our best citizens and employees deserve.

Am I afraid of my government? Indeed. I am afraid that many government leaders have lost sight of what makes us uniquely American. I am afraid that our politicians have lost sight of what role government *should* play in our lives and have acted as if that role should be increased no matter the consequences. We are witnessing the legislative and executive branches display an unquenched thirst for more regulation of the workplace, more control over businesses, and more redirection of profits to those who did not earn them. The trends are disturbing. We have spent hundreds of billions of dollars through stimulus packages, bailouts, and company purchases, all designed to rescue our economy and create jobs, only to see the ranks of the unemployed keep growing, with no end in sight. It is evident their tactics are, at best, stimulating very little true recovery and, at worst, deepening the recession and actually creating further unemployment. Their inept attempts at reviving the economy by throwing hundreds of billions of taxpayer dollars at "too large to fail" businesses have done nothing to re-employ our workers or create jobs. Unless Congress, the courts, and the executive branch discontinue this excessive intrusion in the workplace and in our nation's businesses, then they must be exposed for who they really are: Job Killers.

www.ingramcontent.com/pod-product-compliance
Lightning Source LLC
Chambersburg PA
CBHW051448280526
45785CB00003B/1479

* 9 7 8 1 4 5 0 2 1 0 5 7 7 *